Practice Tests
for Kendall's

Sociology in Our Times
The Essentials
Third Edition

Stephen C. Light
State University of New York at Plattsburgh

WADSWORTH

THOMSON LEARNING

Australia • Canada • Mexico • Singapore • Spain • United Kingdom • United States

COPYRIGHT © 2002 Wadsworth Group. Wadsworth, is an imprint of the Wadsworth Group, a division of Thomson Learning, Inc. Thomson Learning™ is a trademark used herein under license.

ALL RIGHTS RESERVED. No part of this work covered by the copyright hereon may be reproduced or used in any form or by any means—graphic, electronic, or mechanical, including photocopying, recording, taping, Web distribution, or information storage and retrieval systems—without the prior written permission of the publisher.

Printed in the United States of America

1 2 3 4 5 6 7 04 03 02 01 00

For permission to use material from this text, contact us by **Web**: http://www.thomsonrights.com
Fax: 1-800-730-2215 **Phone:** 1-800-730-2214

For more information, contact
Wadsworth/Thomson Learning
10 Davis Drive
Belmont, CA 94002-3098
USA

For more information about our products, contact us:
Thomson Learning Academic Resource Center
1-800-423-0563
http://www.wadsworth.com

International Headquarters
Thomson Learning
International Division
290 Harbor Drive, 2nd Floor
Stamford, CT 06902-7477
USA

UK/Europe/Middle East/South Africa
Thomson Learning
Berkshire House
168-173 High Holborn
London WC1V 7AA
United Kingdom

Asia
Thomson Learning
60 Albert Complex, #15-01
Singapore 189969

Canada
Nelson Thomson Learning
1120 Birchmount Road
Toronto, Ontario M1K 5G4
Canada

ISBN 0-534-57900-0

Contents

Preface

Dear Student,

Welcome to the Practice Tests for Diana Kendall's *Sociology in Our Times: The Essentials*, Third Edition. This book was designed to help you test and apply your knowledge of chapter concepts as you read the textbook and prepare for examinations. Used in conjunction with the third edition Study Guide for *Sociology in Our Times: The Essentials*, this book can be a valuable tool to reinforce your understanding of sociology at the introductory level. Each chapter of the Practice Tests contains 75 multiple-choice questions and 15 True/False questions as well as an answer key. Use the page references in the answer key to revisit the text for information on any questions that you may have missed. Good luck, and enjoy the study of sociology!

Stephen C. Light

Chapter 1
The Sociological Perspective and Research Process

Multiple Choice Questions

1. _____ is the systematic study of human society and social interaction.
   a. Sociology
   b. Psychology
   c. Anthropology
   d. History

2. A(n) _____ is a large social grouping that shares the same geographical territory and is subject to the same political authority and dominant cultural expectations.
   a. interest group
   b. culture
   c. society
   d. ethnic group

3. Sociology is systematic because sociologists apply _____ and _____.
   a. theoretical perspectives, research
   b. common sense, research
   c. common sense, theoretical perspectives
   d. order, stability

4. Environmental problems are an example of the intertwined nature of peoples' lives, and they show how one nation's problems are part of a larger global problem. This relationship between the world's peoples is referred to as _____.
   a. ethnocentrism
   b. global interdependence
   c. cultural expectations
   d. the biosphere

5. According to your text, common sense knowledge is _____.
   a. often a myth
   b. usually based on theory
   c. often based on research
   d. almost always true

6. A(n) _____ is a popular but false notion that may be used, either intentionally or unintentionally, to perpetuate certain beliefs or "theories" even in the light of conclusive evidence to the contrary.
   a. finding
   b. hypothesis
   c. experience
   d. myth

7. Sociologists use _____ to study society and social interaction.
    a. myths
    b. scientific standards
    c. hearsay
    d. common sense ideas

8. In studying groups of people, sociologists look for _____.
    a. patterns
    b. individual explanations
    c. personal troubles
    d. exceptions

9. According to C. Wright Mills, the sociological imagination allows us to see the links between personal troubles and _____.
    a. personal issues
    b. private concerns
    c. public policy
    d. public issues

10. According to early sociologist Emile Durkheim, suicide is caused by _____.
    a. lack of cohesiveness in society
    b. lack of moral standards in society
    c. laws that are too lenient
    d. peoples' individual situations

11. According to your text, the high suicide rate among the Kaiowá Indians in Brazil is related to _____.
    a. their high-income status
    b. loss of their land
    c. losses from earthquakes
    d. their adoption of American cultural values

12. _____ is a term used by many people to specify groups of people distinguished by physical characteristics such as skin color.
    a. Race
    b. Ethnicity
    c. Class
    d. Gender

13. _____ refers to the cultural heritage or identity of a group and is based on factors such as language or country of origin.
    a. Race
    b. Ethnicity
    c. Class
    d. Gender

14. _____ refers to the meanings, beliefs, and practices associated with differences between males and females.
    a. Gender
    b. Sex
    c. Class
    d. Race

15. Which of the following refers to beliefs about behaviors that are seen as appropriate for men (as opposed to women) to engage in?
    a. ethnicity
    b. masculinity
    c. anatomical sex differences
    d. feminism

16. Two processes created social upheavals that led to the systematic study of society in the 19th century. These processes were _____ and _____.
    a. religion, politics
    b. politics, industrialization
    c. industrialization, urbanization
    d. urbanization, morality

17. One of the effects of urbanization is that _____.
    a. the number of industrial jobs declines
    b. people move to rural areas to live
    c. crime rates begin to go down
    d. people change from producers to consumers

18. The term *sociology* was coined by _____, who is commonly known as the founder of sociology as a field of study.
    a. Emile Durkheim
    b. August Comte
    c. Herbert Spencer
    d. Charles Darwin

19. August Comte advocated the philosophy known as _____, which is a belief that the world can best be understood through scientific inquiry.
    a. nihilism
    b. positivism
    c. social Darwinism
    d. scientology

20. August Comte believed that sociology must be _____.
    a. unbiased
    b. religious
    c. feminist
    d. political

21. Nineteenth century British sociologist _____ translated the works of Comte and studied the status of women, children and "sufferers."
    a. Arlie Hochschild
    b. Clara Barton
    c. Harriet Martineau
    d. Agnes Bouvier

22. Which 19th century social theorist is known for his belief that society is best viewed as a biological organism, with various interdependent parts (such as the family, the economy, and government) that work to ensure the stability and survival of the entire society?
    a. Karl Marx
    b. August Comte
    c. Emile Durkheim
    d. Herbert Spencer

23. Which early social theorist is best known for his/her belief that societies grow and change in a process of "survival of the fittest?"
    a. Karl Marx
    b. August Comte
    c. Harriet Martineau
    d. Herbert Spencer

24. The belief that those species of animals, including human beings, that are best adapted to their environment will survive and prosper, whereas those poorly adapted will die out is known as _____.
    a. social Darwinism
    b. Marxism
    c. nihilism
    d. symbolic interactionism

25. Which of the following early social theorists is known for his/her insistence that social facts must be explained by reference to social structure rather than by reference to attributes of individual persons?
    a. Karl Marx
    b. Mary Wollstonecraft
    c. Max Weber
    d. Emile Durkheim

26. Durkheim believed that breakdowns in a society's traditional organization, values, and authority result from _____.
    a. strains
    b. group conflict
    c. differential association
    d. liberalism

27. _____ is a condition in which social control becomes ineffective as a result of the loss of shared values and the loss of a sense of purpose in society.
    a. Functionalism
    b. Culture shock
    c. Cultural relativism
    d. Anomie

28. Durkheim's approach examined the structure of society, but he has been criticized for neglecting the role of _____.
    a. order
    b. agency
    c. anomie
    d. functions

29. Durkheim's approach examined the sources of social stability–the "problem of order"– how society can establish and maintain social stability and cohesiveness. Because of this perspective, Durkheim has been criticized for ignoring the importance of _____.
    a. subjective meaning
    b. structure
    c. functions
    d. anomic suicide

30. Which of the following persons is *not* considered to be one of the key figures in the early development of social theory and/or research?
    a. Karl Marx
    b. Emile Durkheim
    c. Louis Pasteur
    d. Harriet Martineau

31. Which of the following social theorists is best known for his belief that history is a continuous clash between conflicting ideas and forces?
    a. Karl Marx
    b. Emile Durkheim
    c. Robert Merton
    d. Georg Simmel

32. According to German social thinker Karl Marx, which of the following social institutions is most important in determining the structure of societies?
    a. the family
    b. religion
    c. the economy
    d. government

33. According to Karl Marx, history is a product of the struggle between _____.
   a. religions
   b. national governments
   c. family groups
   d. social classes

34. Karl Marx believed that capitalism is characterized by conflict between _____.
   a. owners and workers
   b. managers and owners
   c. managers and workers
   d. labor unions and owners

35. Karl Marx referred to the owners of a society's means of production as the _____.
   a. proletariat
   b. cultural elite
   c. bourgeoisie
   d. chosen ones

36. Karl Marx referred to the social class made up of persons who work for wages as the _____.
   a. proletariat
   b. cultural elite
   c. bourgeoisie
   d. working poor

37. According to Karl Marx, the capitalist class pays workers less than the value of their labor. This results in a feeling of _____ among the workers.
   a. usefulness
   b. alienation
   c. duty
   d. power

38. According to Karl Marx, once members of the working class become aware of the extent to which they are being exploited, they will _____.
   a. form labor unions
   b. establish a classless society
   c. cheat on their taxes
   d. ask the government for more money

39. German social scientist Max Weber believed that sociology should be _____.
   a. subjective
   b. value laden
   c. unscientific
   d. value free

6

40. Max Weber agreed with Karl Marx that _____ is an important social institution, but he disagreed with Marx's contention that it was more important than the other social institutions.
    a. the family
    b. the educational system
    c. religion
    d. the economy

41. Max Weber is best known for his study of _____.
    a. bureaucracy
    b. communal living
    c. warfare
    d. aging and death

42. According to Max Weber, the most significant factor in determining the social relations between people in industrial societies is _____.
    a. class struggle
    b. rational bureaucracy
    c. symbolic interaction
    d. culture shock

43. Which of the following social theorists concluded that interaction patterns differ according to the size of the group?
    a. Karl Marx
    b. Harriet Martineau
    c. Emile Durkheim
    d. Georg Simmel

44. Georg Simmel adopted an approach that focuses attention on the universal recurring social forms that underlie the varying content of social life. Simmel's approach is known as _____.
    a. formal sociology
    b. classicism
    c. conflict sociology
    d. status quo sociology

45. The first departments of sociology in the United States were located at The University of Chicago and _____.
    a. Harvard University
    b. Yale University
    c. The University of California at Berkeley
    d. Atlanta University

46.	Which of the following persons was founder of Hull House in Chicago, and later won the Nobel Prize for work with the underprivileged?
	a.	Robert E. Park
	b.	George Herbert Mead
	c.	Jane Addams
	d.	Harriet Martineau

47.	Which of the following persons founded the department of sociology at Atlanta University, which was the second such department to be created in the United States?
	a.	Robert E. Park
	b.	George Herbert Mead
	c.	Jane Addams
	d.	W.E.B. Du Bois

48.	W.E.B. Du Bois was one of the first scholars to note that a dual heritage creates conflict for people of color in the United States. He called this duality _____, which is the identity conflict of being a Black and an American.
	a.	role strain
	b.	double-consciousness
	c.	double trouble
	d.	identity strain

49.	W.E.B. Du Bois noted that Americans espouse such values as democracy, freedom, and equality, but at the same time they accept _____.
	a.	meritocracy
	b.	education
	c.	pluralism
	d.	racism

50.	A(n) _____ is a set of logically interrelated statements that attempts to describe, explain, and (occasionally) predict social events.
	a.	theory
	b.	hypothesis
	c.	observation
	d.	conclusion

51.	Which of the following theoretical perspectives is based on the assumption that society is a stable, orderly system?
	a.	the functionalist perspective
	b.	the conflict perspective
	c.	the symbolic interactionist perspective
	d.	the postmodern perspective

52. The functionalist perspective assumes that a majority of society's members share a common set of values, beliefs, and behavioral expectations. This is referred to as _____.
    a. parsimony
    b. symbolism
    c. societal consensus
    d. societal agreement

53. According to the functionalist perspective, each social institution (family, education, government, religion, the economy) _____.
    a. serves a function
    b. creates group conflict
    c. is based on symbols
    d. is unreal

54. According to sociologist Robert K. Merton, _____ are functions of a social institution that are intended and overtly recognized by participants in a social unit.
    a. manifest functions
    b. latent functions
    c. consequent functions
    d. inconsequent functions

55. According to sociologist Robert K. Merton, _____ are unintended functions that are hidden and remain unacknowledged by participants.
    a. manifest functions
    b. latent functions
    c. consequent functions
    d. inconsequent functions

56. Sociologist Donna Gaines analyzed the suicide pact of four New Jersey teenagers, from a functionalist perspective. She concluded that Durkheim's category of *anomic suicide* applies to the teenagers' actions because they _____.
    a. felt that they had no meaningful choices in life
    b. believed in a glorious afterlife in Heaven
    c. wanted to make a political statement
    d. did not feel connected to society

57. Which of the following theoretical perspectives assumes that society is made up of groups of people who are engaged in a continuous power struggle for control of scarce resources?
    a. the functionalist perspective
    b. the conflict perspective
    c. the symbolic interactionist perspective
    d. the postmodern perspective

58.   _____ believed that value-free sociology is impossible because sociologists must make value-related choices in the topics they investigate and the theoretical approaches they adopt.
       a.   Emile Durkheim
       b.   Georg Simmel
       c.   August Comte
       d.   C. Wright Mills

59.   Neo-Marxist theory and the feminist perspective are both branches of _____ theory.
       a.   functionalist
       b.   conflict
       c.   symbolic interactionist
       d.   postmodern

60.   According to the feminist perspective, _____ is socially created, rather than determined by one's biological inheritance.
       a.   sex
       b.   gender
       c.   disease
       d.   physical strength

61.   According to feminists, we live in a society that is organized to systematically favor men over women in all aspects of life. This type of society is referred to as a _____.
       a.   conflict society
       b.   matriarchy
       c.   patriarchy
       d.   gender structure

62.   Which of the following social scientists was most instrumental in developing the theoretical perspective known as *symbolic interactionism*?
       a.   Robert E. Park
       b.   George Herbert Mead
       c.   Jane Addams
       d.   W.E.B. Du Bois

63.   Which of the following theoretical perspectives adopts a *microlevel* approach?
       a.   functionalism
       b.   conflict theory
       c.   symbolic interactionism
       d.   postmodern theory

64. According to the _____ theoretical perspective, society is the sum of interactions of people and groups.
   a. functionalist
   b. conflict
   c. symbolic interactionist
   d. postmodern

65. The _____ perspective assumes that "reality" is not necessarily shared by others. Instead, definitions of reality are acquired and shared through agreed-upon symbols such as language.
   a. functionalist
   b. conflict
   c. symbolic interactionist
   d. postmodern

66. According to the symbolic interactionist perspective, many suicide attempts may be _____.
   a. a search for relief of pain
   b. a lazy way out
   c. based on religious motives
   d. a cry for help

67. Which of the following theoretical perspectives challenges all of the other perspectives and questions current belief systems?
   a. functionalism
   b. conflict theory
   c. symbolic interactionism
   d. postmodern theory

68. Which of the following techniques of conducting research is defined as a poll where the researcher gathers facts or attempts to determine the relationship among facts?
   a. survey
   b. experiment
   c. analysis of existing data
   d. field research

69. One advantage of _____ is that it tends to produce uniform or replicable data that can be elicited time after time by different interviewers.
   a. the unstructured interview
   b. the structured interview
   c. field research
   d. secondary analysis

70. Statistical analysis that simultaneously examines more than two independent variables is referred to as _____.
    a. univariate analysis
    b. multivariate analysis
    c. qualitative analysis
    d. field research

71. _____ is the systematic examination of cultural artifacts or various forms of communication to extract thematic data and draw conclusions about social life.
    a. Cultural relativism
    b. Monotheism
    c. Quantitative analysis
    d. Content analysis

72. The method of field research known as _____ involves a process of collecting systematic observations while the researcher is being part of the activities of the group that is being studied.
    a. content analysis
    b. experimentation
    c. participant observation
    d. detached observation

73. If 1) a correlation exists between two variables, 2) the independent variable occurred prior to the dependent variable, and 3) any change in the dependent variable is not due to a variable which is outside the stated hypothesis, then we can say that _____.
    a. the research study should be repeated
    b. a cause-and-effect relationship exists
    c. quantitative analysis is called for
    d. our theory is incorrect

74. The major advantage of _____ is the researcher's control over the environment and the ability to isolate the experimental variable.
    a. a survey
    b. an experiment
    c. field research
    d. participant observation

75. According to your textbook, sociological researchers are ethically required to _____.
    a. obtain the informed consent of research subjects
    b. publish research subjects' full names whenever possible
    c. pay all research subjects for participating in the study
    d. report unethical behavior by research subjects to the authorities

True-False Questions

1.   Common sense beliefs are always correct.

2.   Widespread unemployment as a result of economic changes such as factory closings is an example of a *private trouble*.

3.   Herbert Spencer's notion of *the survival of the fittest* can easily be used to justify class, racial-ethnic, and gender inequalities.

4.   According to C. Wright Mills, the most important decisions in the United States are made largely behind the scenes by a small group of officials he called *the power elite*.

5.   According to the feminist perspective, American men and women have now achieved approximately equal access to scarce resources such as wealth, prestige, and power.

6.   In North America, women are more likely to attempt suicide than men, but men are more likely to actually succeed in taking their own life.

7.   A group with one of the lowest suicide rates in North America is young Native American males who live on government reservations.

8.   According to the symbolic interactionist perspective, a symbol is anything that meaningfully represents something else.

9.   When one is conducting a research project using the conventional model of research, it is necessary to conduct a review of previous research on the topic.

10.   A *unit of analysis* is what or whom is being studied.

11.   According to your textbook, data must be analyzed using statistics.

12.   Depending on the purpose of the particular research, scholars can choose to use either quantitative or qualitative methods of analysis.

13.   The best type of data collection to use if one is interested in comparing two groups, one of which has received a certain treatment and the other of which has not, is the *experiment*.

14.   *Secondary analysis* requires researchers to collect data from two different groups.

15.   A *correlation* exists when two variables are associated more frequently than could be expected by chance.

Chapter 1: Answers to Practice Test Questions

(question-answer-page number)

Multiple Choice Questions

1. a 3
2. c 3
3. a 3
4. b 3
5. a 3
6. d 3
7. b 3
8. a 3
9. d 4
10. a 4
11. b 8
12. a 8
13. b 8
14. a 8
15. b 8
16. c 8
17. d 9
18. b 9
19. b 10
20. a 10
21. c 21
22. d 11
23. d 11
24. a 11
25. d 12
26. a 12
27. d 12
28. b 12
29. a 12
30. c 12
31. a 13
32. c 12
33. d 13
34. a 13
35. c 13
36. a 13
37. b 13
38. b 13
39. d 13
40. d 13

41. a 13
42. b 13
43. d 14
44. a 14
45. d 14
46. c 14
47. d 15
48. b 15
49. d 15
50. a 15
51. a 15
52. c 15
53. a 16
54. a 16
55. b 16
56. a 16
57. b 16
58. d 17
59. b 17
60. b 17
61. c 17
62. b 18
63. c 18
64. c 18
65. c 19
66. d 19
67. d 20
68. a 28
69. b 29
70. b 29
71. d 30
72. c 31
73. b 32
74. b 32
75. a 32

True-False Questions

1. F 5
2. F 4
3. T 12
4. T 17
5. F 17

6. T 18
7. F 18
8. T 19
9. T 22
10. T 24
11. F 27
12. T 27
13. T 32
14. F 30
15. T 32

Chapter 2
Culture

Multiple Choice Questions

1. A _____ is a large social grouping that occupies the same geographic territory and is subject to the same political authority and dominant cultural expectations.
   a. subculture
   b. minority group
   c. culture
   d. society

2. A _____ is the knowledge, language, values, customs, and material objects that are passed from person to person and from one generation to the next in a human group or society.
   a. subculture
   b. minority group
   c. culture
   d. society

3. Children who are _____ have a "third culture"–they share neither their parents' culture nor the cultures in which they have lived, but rather have a combination of cultures.
   a. ethnic refugees
   b. global nomads
   c. world travelers
   d. stateless persons

4. Making a circle with your thumb and index finger indicates "OK" in the United States, but in Tunisia it means _____.
   a. "You have a phone call"
   b. "Your father has a bad reputation"
   c. "I'll kill you"
   d. "Bring the car around"

5. Sociologists believe that most, if not all, of human behavior is determined by _____ (our social environment) rather than _____ (our biological and genetic makeup).
   a. nature, nurture
   b. nurture, nature
   c. nature, culture
   d. culture, society

6. A _____ is an unlearned, biologically determined involuntary response to some physical stimuli (such as a sneeze after breathing pepper).
    a. reflex
    b. drive
    c. behavior
    d. complex response

7. _____ are unlearned, biologically determined impulses common to all members of a species that satisfy needs such as those for sleep, food, water, or sexual gratification.
    a. Reflexes
    b. Drives
    c. Instincts
    d. Complex responses

8. Which of the following is NOT an example of material culture?
    a. a political system
    a. an automobile
    b. technology
    c. a cathedral

9. Initially, items of material culture begin as raw materials or resources such as ore, trees, and oil. Through _____, these raw materials are transformed into usable items.
    a. nonmaterial culture
    b. cultural universals
    c. technology
    d. language

10. _____ are customs and practices that occur across all societies.
    a. Instincts
    b. Cultural universals
    c. Cultural artifacts
    d. Diversity rules

11. Which of the following is NOT an example of a cultural universal?
    a. bodily adornment, including hairstyles
    b. telling jokes
    c. cooking food
    d. wearing blue jeans

12. All cultures have four nonmaterial cultural components. Which of the following is NOT one of the four nonmaterial components of culture?
    a. symbols
    b. norms
    c. values
    d. gifts

13. _____ is a set of symbols that expresses ideas and enables people to think and communicate with one another.
    a. Education
    b. Morality
    c. Language
    d. Personality

14. In a study of baby clothing, Sociologist Madeline Shakin and her associates found that _____ percent of infants were dressed in colors indicating their sex.
    a. 30
    b. 50
    c. 60
    d. 90

15. Which of the following statements best reflects the main point of the Sapir-Whorf hypothesis?
    a. There are no true races. The concept of race is biologically meaningless.
    b. Language shapes the view of reality of its speakers.
    c. Some cultural practices such as joking are found in every human society.
    d. The Confederate flag is considered by some to be a symbol of hatred.

16. Which of the following statements is NOT consistent with the Sapir-Whorf hypothesis?
    a. The English language ignores women by using "man" in words (such as "chairman") that include men and women.
    b. People who live in snowy climates have many words for snow.
    c. People tend to perceive reality in the same way, regardless of the language they speak.
    d. Words like "fox," "broad," and "bitch" reinforce the idea that women are sexual objects.

17. Pronouns show the gender of the person we expect to be in a particular occupation. For instance, _____ are usually referred to as "she".
    a. schoolteachers
    b. engineers
    c. presidents
    d. electricians

18. Which of the following is an example of sexist language?
    a. bachelor
    b. teacher
    c. doctor
    d. prostitute

19. Which of the following is a genderless title?
    a. stewardess
    b. firefighter
    c. actress
    d. Congressman

20. According to the _____ theoretical perspective, a shared language is essential to a common culture; language is a stabilizing force in society.
    a. functionalist
    b. conflict
    c. symbolic interactionist
    d. feminist

21. In the 1990's, more than _____ percent of all U.S. residents age 5 and older spoke a language other than English at home.
    a. 7
    b. 14
    c. 23
    d. 41

22. Which of the following statements best reflects the assumptions of functionalist theory?
    a. Language is a stabilizing force in society.
    b. Language reflects a society's existing power relations.
    c. The categories of language shape people's views of reality.
    d. Many languages are no longer being spoken in the home.

23. Latinos/as in New Mexico use _____, which are proverbs or sayings that are unique to the Spanish language.
    a. *ochos*
    b. *burritos*
    c. *dichos*
    d. *casas*

24. _____ theorists view language as a source of power and social control; it perpetuates inequalities between people and between groups because words are used (whether intentionally or unintentionally) to "keep people in their place."
    a. Functionalist
    b. Conflict
    c. Symbolic Interactionist
    d. Postmodern

25. _____ are collective ideas about what is right or wrong, good or bad, and desirable or undesirable in a particular culture.
   a.   Values
   b.   Conformities
   c.   Societies
   d.   Sanctions

26. Which of the following theoretical perspectives assumes that shared values are essential for societies?
   a.   functionalist theory
   b.   conflict theory
   c.   symbolic interactionist theory
   d.   postmodern theory

27. Sociologist Robin Williams has identified a set of core American values. Which of the following is NOT one of the core American values mentioned by Williams?
   a.   thriftiness
   b.   equality
   c.   progress and material comfort
   d.   racism and group superiority

28. _____ are values that conflict with one another or are mutually exclusive (achieving one makes it difficult, if not impossible, to achieve another).
   a.   Social mores
   b.   Role conflicts
   c.   Prescriptive norms
   d.   Value contradictions

29. _____ refers to the values and standards of behavior that people in a society profess to hold, while _____ refers to the values and standards of behavior that people actually follow.
   a.   Real culture, ideal culture
   b.   Ideal culture, real culture
   c.   Culture, society
   d.   Society, value contradictions

30. _____ are established rules of behavior or standards of conduct.
   a.   Fashions
   b.   Norms
   c.   Values
   d.   Sanctions

31. Which of the following type of social norms usually receives the least serious reaction from people, when the norm is violated?
    a. folkways
    a. mores
    b. taboos
    c. laws

32. Which of the following is an example of a more?
    a. not tying one's shoelace
    b. not standing too close to others when speaking to them
    c. the requirement that motorists stop at traffic lights
    d. the expectation that parents will provide food for their children

33. _____ are rewards for appropriate behavior or penalties for inappropriate behavior.
    a. Medals
    b. Punishments
    c. Sanctions
    d. Norms

34. _____ is an example of a taboo that is nearly universal across the world's cultures.
    a. Sex between partners of the opposite sex
    b. Sex between partners of the same sex
    c. Sex between older persons and younger persons
    d. Sex between persons who are closely related to each other

35. The death penalty is an example of a _____ that is administered for violating the criminal law.
    a. sanction
    b. more
    c. folkway
    d. value contradiction

36. The _____ law deals with disputes among persons or groups, and may result in negative sanctions such as having to pay compensation or being ordered to stop the conduct.
    a. civil
    b. criminal
    c. regulatory
    d. domestic

37. When _____ laws are violated, fines and prison sentences are the most likely negative sanctions, although in some states the death penalty is handed down for certain offenses.
   a. civil
   b. criminal
   c. regulatory
   d. domestic

38. _____ are formal, standardized norms that have been enacted by legislatures and are enforced by formal sanctions.
   a. Folkways
   b. Mores
   c. Taboos
   d. Laws

39. Which of the following is an example of a folkway in the United States?
   a. using underarm deodorant
   b. stopping at a stop sign
   c. filing a tax return
   d. not eating human body parts for dinner

40. _____ refers to the knowledge, techniques, and tools that allow people to transform resources into usable forms, and the knowledge and skills required to use what is developed.
   a. Education
   b. Training
   c. Technology
   d. Pedagogy

41. Which of the following is an example of a *new technology*?
   a. invention of the printing press
   b. upgraded computer software
   c. the latest model Ford automobile
   d. an airplane that holds more people than previous models

42. _____ occurs when material culture changes faster than nonmaterial culture.
   a. Cultural diversity
   b. Cultural plurality
   c. Cultural acceleration
   d. Cultural lag

43. The author of your textbook suggests that even though the technology now exists to create a national computerized data bank that would include everyone's medical history from birth to death, this does not mean that such a data bank will be accepted by people who believe that it would constitute an unacceptable invasion of privacy. This situation is an example of _____.
   a.   cultural diversity
   b.   cultural plurality
   c.   cultural acceleration
   d.   cultural lag

44. According to your textbook, cultural changes are often set in motion by three processes. Which of the following is NOT one of the three processes discussed in the text?
   a.   discovery
   b.   invention
   c.   stasis
   d.   diffusion

45. _____ is the transmission of cultural items or social practices from one group or society to another through such means as exploration, military endeavors, the media, tourism, and immigration.
   a.   Discovery
   b.   Invention
   c.   Stasis
   d.   Diffusion

46. _____ is the process of reshaping existing cultural items into a new form. Examples include guns, video games, airplanes, and First Amendment rights.
   a.   Discovery
   b.   Invention
   c.   Exploration
   d.   Diffusion

47. *Piñatas* were first brought from China by Marco Polo. They found their way to Italy, Spain, and then Mexico, where they were used to celebrate the birth of the Aztec god Huitzilopochtli. This is an example of _____.
   a.   technology
   b.   cultural lag
   c.   diffusion
   d.   cultural diversity

48. There is often a wide range of cultural differences found between and within nations. These differences are referred to as _____.
   a.   cultural diversity
   b.   immigrant pluralism
   c.   Affirmative Action
   d.   ethnocentrism

49. A(n) _____ is a category of people who share distinguishing attributes, beliefs, values, and/or norms that set them apart in some significant manner from the dominant culture.
   a. interest group
   b. subculture
   c. society
   d. cohort

50. Nations such as Sweden, which include people who share a common culture and are typically from similar social, religious, political, and economic backgrounds, are referred to as _____ societies.
   a. homogeneous
   b. heterogeneous
   c. limited
   d. ethnocentric

51. _____ societies include people who are dissimilar in regard to social characteristics such as religion, income, or race/ethnicity.
   a. Homogeneous
   b. Heterogeneous
   c. Limited
   d. Ethnocentric

52. The Old Order Amish first arrived in the United States in the early 1700s, and they have fought to preserve their distinct identity ever since. The Old Order Amish illustrate the concept of _____.
   a. interest group
   b. subculture
   c. society
   d. cohort

53. In the United States, Native Americans, Muslims, Generation Xers and motorcycle enthusiasts are examples of _____.
   a. heterogenous groups
   b. subcultures
   c. countercultures
   d. cohorts

54. A _____ is a group that strongly rejects dominant societal values and norms and seeks alternative lifestyles.
   a. religion
   b. subculture
   c. counterculture
   d. ethnic group

55.   _____ is the disorientation that people feel when they encounter cultures radically different from their own.
    a.   Ethnocentrism
    b.   Cultural relativity
    c.   Cultural imperialism
    d.   Culture shock

56.   The Ku Klux Klan, neo-Nazi skinheads, the beatniks of the 1950s, and the flower children of the 1960s are examples of _____.
    a.   religions
    b.   subcultures
    c.   countercultures
    d.   ethnic groups

57.   When people travel to another society, they may not know how to respond to that setting, and they may believe that they cannot depend on their taken-for-granted assumptions about life. This reaction is called _____.
    a.   culture shock
    b.   cultural barriers
    c.   culture conflict
    d.   ethnocentrism

58.   Sometimes people use their own culture as the yardstick by which they judge the behavior of persons from another culture. This practice is known as _____.
    a.   cultural pluralism
    b.   subcultural lag
    c.   culture conflict
    d.   ethnocentrism

59.   _____ is based on the assumption that one's own way of life is superior to all others.
    a.   cultural pluralism
    b.   subcultural lag
    c.   culture conflict
    d.   ethnocentrism

60.   Social scientists teach us that the behaviors and customs of any culture must be viewed and analyzed by that culture's own standards. This is known as _____.
    a.   ethnocentrism
    b.   cultural relativism
    c.   cultural pluralism
    d.   secular humanism

61. French sociologist Pierre Bourdieu's (1984) *cultural capital theory* views _____ as a device used by the dominant class to exclude the subordinate classes.
   a. popular culture
   b. high culture
   c. the Internet
   d. retirement accounts

62. _____ consists of activities, products, and services that are assumed to appeal primarily to members of the middle and working classes.
   a. Popular culture
   b. High culture
   c. Functional assets
   d. The Gross National Product

63. Which of the following is NOT an example of high culture?
   a. the opera
   b. ballet
   c. television
   d. classical music

64. Three prevalent forms of popular culture are discussed in the text. Which of the following is NOT one of the three?
   a. fads
   b. fashions
   c. leisure activities
   d. theater productions

65. According to sociologist John Lofland, fads can be divided into four categories. Which of the following types of fad is illustrated by Beanie Babies, characters from the movie Star Wars, toys, trading cards, clothing, cartoons, and snacks?
   a. object fads
   b. activity fads
   c. idea fads
   d. personality fads

66. According to sociologist John Lofland, fads can be divided into four categories. Which of the following types of fad is illustrated by body piercing and surfing the Internet?
   a. object fads
   b. activity fads
   c. idea fads
   d. personality fads

67. A _____ is a currently valued style of behavior, thinking, or appearance that is longer lasting and more widespread than a fad.
    a. culture
    b. fluke
    c. universal
    d. fashion

68. Which of the following theoretical perspectives views values and norms (components of culture) as means of creating and sustaining the privileged position of the powerful in society while excluding others?
    a. functionalist theory
    b. conflict theory
    c. symbolic interactionist theory
    d. postmodern theory

69. Which of the following theoretical perspectives views culture as the "glue" that holds society together?
    a. functionalist theory
    b. conflict theory
    c. symbolic interactionist theory
    d. postmodern theory

70. Which of the following theoretical perspectives assumes that ideas, a nonmaterial component of culture, are used by agents of the ruling class (or classes) to affect the thoughts and actions of members of other classes?
    a. functionalist theory
    b. conflict theory
    c. symbolic interactionist theory
    d. postmodern theory

71. _____ are objects outside ourselves that we purchase to satisfy our human needs or wants.
    a. Cultures
    b. Commodities
    c. Stocks
    d. Extrinsics

72. Classical sociologist Georg Simmel suggested that people initially create money as a means of exchange, but then money acquires a social meaning that extends beyond its purely economic functions. Simmel's views are closest to the _____ theoretical perspective.
    a. functionalist
    b. conflict
    c. symbolic interactionist
    d. postmodern

73. _____ theorists believe that much of what has been written about culture in the Western world is Eurocentric–that it is based on the uncritical assumption that European culture is the true, universal culture in which all of the world's people ought to believe.
    a. Functionalist
    b. Conflict
    c. Symbolic interactionist
    d. Postmodern

74. According to the view of _____ theorists, no one authority can claim to know social reality, and we should deconstruct existing beliefs and theories about culture in hopes of gaining new insights.
    a. functionalist
    b. conflict
    c. symbolic interactionist
    d. postmodern

75. The importance of multicultural education is illustrated by the fact that in the Los Angeles school district, students speak more than _____ different languages and dialects.
    a. 58
    a. 114
    b. 160
    c. 198

True-False Questions

1. Society and culture are interdependent; neither could exist without the other.

2. The U.S. Constitution designates English as the official language of this country.

3. Core values in the United States include racism and a belief in the superiority of one's own group.

4. Some individuals are born with hatred for people who are different from themselves.

5. As the United States is increasing in diversity, most dominant-group members are becoming more tolerant of social and cultural diversity.

6. Hand gestures (such as forming a circle with the thumb and index finger) generally have the same meaning in all of the world's cultures.

7. Because of "human nature," humans are born knowing how to express kindness and hatred toward others.

8. Some form of rule making and rule enforcing exists in all societies.

9.   Human beings have instincts.

10.   Most modern sociologists believe that culture and social learning, not nature, account for virtually all of our behavior patterns.

11.   Religion is a cultural universal.

12.   According to your textbook, language is not solely a human characteristic. Other animals use sounds, gestures, touch, and smell to communicate with one another, but humans have a unique ability to manipulate symbols to express abstract concepts.

13.   Researchers have found that chimpanzees can use elements of American Sign Language and they can manipulate objects to make "sentences."

14.   According to sociologist Robin Williams, some American core values contradict other American core values.

15.   According to the textbook, societies continually experience cultural change.

Chapter 2: Answers to Practice Test Questions

(question-answer-page)

Multiple Choice Questions

1. d 38
2. c 38
3. b 38
4. c 41
5. b 42
6. a 42
7. b 42
8. a 42
9. c 42
10. b 43
11. d 43
12. d 45
13. c 46
14. d 46
15. b 47
16. c 47
17. a 47
18. a 48
19. b 48
20. a 49
21. b 49
22. a 49
23. c 50
24. b 50
25. a 50
26. a 51
27. a 51
28. d 52
29. b 52
30. b 52
31. a 53
32. d 53
33. c 53
34. d 53
35. a 53
36. a 53
37. b 53
38. d 53
39. a 53
40. c 54

41. a 54
42. d 54
43. d 54
44. c 54
45. d 54
46. b 54
47. c 54
48. a 54
49. b 55
50. a 55
51. b 55
52. b 57
53. b 57
54. c 58
55. d 58
56. c 58
57. a 59
58. d 59
59. d 59
60. b 60
61. b 60
62. a 60
63. c 60
64. d 61
65. a 61
66. b 61
67. d 61
68. b 62
69. a 62
70. b 64
71. b 64
72. c 65
73. d 65
74. d 66
75. b 66

True-False Questions

1. T 38
2. F 39
3. T 39
4. F 39
5. F 39

6. F 41
7. F 40
8. T 41
9. F 42
10. T 42
11. T 44
12. T 47
13. T 46
14. T 52
15. T 54

Chapter 3
Socialization

Multiple Choice Questions

1.   _____ is the lifelong process of social interaction through which individuals acquire a self-identity and the physical, mental, and social skills needed for survival in society.
   a.   Culture
   b.   Society
   c.   Socialization
   d.   Sociobiology

2.   Which of the following theoretical perspectives assumes that socialization is necessary in order for a society to "reproduce" itself by passing on its culture from one generation to the next?
   a.   functionalist theory
   b.   conflict theory
   c.   symbolic interactionist theory
   d.   feminist theory

3.   The socialization process is most effective when people conform to the norms of society because _____.
   a.   of the existence of police
   b.   of the sanctions they might experience if they do not conform
   c.   they believe that this is the best course of action
   d.   they feel that society might fall apart if they did not conform

4.   The _____ socialization differ(s) greatly from society to society.
   a.   content of
   b.   concept of
   c.   need for
   d.   participants in

5.   According to the textbook, annual costs for child care (per child) fall into which of the following ranges in the United States?
   a. $500-$2000
   b. $2000-3000
   c. $3000-6000
   d. $3000-8000

6.   _____ is the systematic study of how biology affects social behavior.
   a.   Sociobiology
   b.   Sociology
   c.   Psychology
   d.   Social psychology

7.   Studies of children who are raised in isolation suggest that _____.
     a.   biological factors are more important that social factors in explaining human behavior
     b.   human children must be exposed to contact with others in order to become fully human
     c.   human children have a remarkable ability to become socialized, even when they are raised in isolation
     d.   children who are not exposed to human speech will create their own language systems

8.   Psychologists Harry and Margaret Harlow conducted a series of laboratory experiments on infant Rhesus monkeys raised in isolation. They found that _____.
     a.   the monkeys preferred wire mother-substitutes over cloth mother-substitutes
     b.   the monkeys exhibited no apparent need for social contact
     c.   the monkeys were unable to relate to other monkeys later on
     d.   the process of socialization was unimportant for the monkeys

9.   The most frequent type of child maltreatment is _____.
     a.   sexual abuse
     b.   neglect of basic needs
     c.   violent abuse and injury
     d.   psychological torture

10.   Which of the following scholars proposed a *psychological* theory of human development?
     a.   Charles Horton Cooley
     b.   Carol Gilligan
     c.   George Herbert Mead
     d.   Emile Durkheim

11.   According to _____, human behavior and personality originate from unconscious forces within individuals.
     a.   Sigmund Freud
     b.   Charles Horton Cooley
     c.   Emile Durkheim
     d.   Jean Piaget

12.   According to Sigmund Freud, the human personality encompasses three components. Which of the following is NOT one of the components of personality that was proposed by Freud?
     a.   id
     b.   ego
     c.   superego
     d.   superid

13. The _____ is the component of personality that includes all of the individual's basic biological drives and needs that demand immediate gratification.
    a. id
    b. ego
    c. superego
    d. unconscious

14. For Sigmund Freud, the newborn child's personality is all _____, which is the urge for immediate gratification.
    a. id
    b. ego
    c. superego
    d. unconscious

15. According to Sigmund Freud, the _____ is the rational, reality-oriented component of personality that imposes restrictions on the innate pleasure-seeking drives of the id.
    a. ego
    b. superego
    c. superid
    d. executive

16. According to Freud, the _____ is the moral and ethical component of personality.
    a. id
    b. ego
    c. superego
    d. superid

17. According to Sigmund Freud's approach, which of the following components of personality is dominant in a well adjusted person? That is, which component successfully manages the opposing forces of the other two components in the mature personality?
    a. id
    b. ego
    c. superego
    d. executive

18. In which of Piaget's levels of development do children understand the world only through sensory contact and immediate action, because they cannot engage in symbolic thought or use language?
    a. sensorimotor stage
    b. preoperational stage
    c. concrete operational stage
    d. formal operational stage

19. In which of Piaget's levels of development do children think in terms of tangible objects and actual events, and begin to take the role of others?
    a. sensorimotor stage
    b. preoperational stage
    c. concrete operational stage
    d. formal operational stage

20. In which of Piaget's levels of development do children begin to use words as mental symbols and to form mental images, but are still limited in their ability to use logic to solve problems?
    a. sensorimotor stage
    b. preoperational stage
    c. concrete operational stage
    d. formal operational stage

21. In which of Piaget's levels of development are children able to engage in highly abstract thought and understand places, things, and events they have never seen?
    a. sensorimotor stage
    b. preoperational stage
    c. concrete operational stage
    d. formal operational stage

22. According to Piaget, children who are in the _____ of cognitive development will be unable to recognize that two different-shaped glasses actually contain the same amount of water.
    a. sensorimotor
    b. preoperational
    c. concrete operational
    d. formal operational

23. Lawrence Kohlberg elaborated on Piaget's theories of cognitive reasoning by conducting a series of studies in which children, adolescents, and adults were presented with moral dilemmas that took the form of _____.
    a. objects of different size
    b. stories
    c. animals and plants
    d. abstract ideas

24. According to Lawrence Kohlberg, people who have developed to the _____ level of moral reasoning judge moral conduct by principles based on human rights that transcend government and laws.
    a. preconventional
    b. conventional
    c. postconventional
    d. extraconventional

25. According to Lawrence Kohlberg, people who have developed to the _____ level of moral reasoning judge behavior to be evil if the behavior is likely to be punished.
    a. preconventional
    b. conventional
    c. postconventional
    d. extraconventional

26. According to Lawrence Kohlberg, people who have developed to the _____ level of moral reasoning are most concerned with how they are perceived by their peers and with how one conforms to rules.
    a. preconventional
    b. conventional
    c. postconventional
    d. extraconventional

27. Psychologist Carol Gilligan argued that Lawrence Kohlberg's theory of moral development is flawed because it ignores the influence of _____ on the way that people think.
    a. race
    b. gender
    c. age
    d. social class

28. According to the sociological perspective on human development, we cannot form a sense of self or personal identity _____.
    a. without contact with others
    b. unless we choose a mate
    c. without religious influences
    d. until about the age of 12

29. Four concepts make up our self-concept: the physical self, the active self, the social self, and _____.
    a. the economic self
    b. the psychological self
    c. the historical self
    d. the unconscious self

30. The words *I, me, my, mine,* and *myself* refer to our _____.
    a. literary ability
    b. psychological traits
    c. sense of self
    d. sense of belonging

31. According to sociologist Charles Horton Cooley, our sense of self is based on our perception of how other people think of us. Cooley referred to this process as the _____.
    a. reflective self
    b. looking-glass self
    c. role self
    d. projected self

32. According to George Herbert Mead, _____ is the process by which a person mentally assumes the role of another person or group in order to understand the world from that person's or group's point of view.
    a. identification
    b. role projection
    c. role making
    d. role taking

33. According to George Herbert Mead, _____ is when a person begins to construct his or her own roles.
    a. identification
    b. role projection
    c. role making
    d. role taking

34. According to George Herbert Mead, _____ are those persons whose care, affection, and approval are especially desired and who are most important in the development of the self.
    a. role models
    b. significant others
    c. mentors
    d. essential personalities

35. George Herbert Mead proposed that children progress through three stages of development. During the _____ stage, children's interactions lack meaning, and children largely imitate the people around them.
    a. preparatory
    b. play
    c. game
    d. model

36. George Herbert Mead proposed that children progress through three stages of development. During the _____ stage, children understand not only their own social position but also the positions of others around them.
    a. preparatory
    b. play
    c. game
    d. model

37. George Herbert Mead used the term _____ to refer to the child's awareness of the demands and expectations of the society as a whole or of the child's subculture.
   a. significant other
   b. role model
   c. generalized other
   d. mentor

38. According to your textbook, _____ are the persons, groups, or institutions that teach us what we need to know in order to participate in society.
   a. key interactants
   b. social nodes
   c. opinion leaders
   d. agents of socialization

39. Symbolic interactionist theorists suggest that a child's self-concept is defined and evaluated through interaction with _____.
   a. key interactants
   b. significant others
   c. opinion leaders
   d. adults

40. The family, the school, peer groups, and the mass media are the most important _____ for persons during their childhood years.
   a. key interactants
   b. social nodes
   c. opinion leaders
   d. agents of socialization

41. Which of the following social institutions is (ideally) the primary source of emotional support, love, understanding, security, acceptance, intimacy, and companionship?
   a. family
   b. education
   c. religion
   d. government

42. According to your textbook, the _____ is the most important agent of socialization in all societies.
   a. family
   b. school
   c. peer group
   d. mass media

43. Sociologist Melvin Kohn has found that the _____ of parents is related to the amount of conformity and obedience that parents expect from their children.
    a. occupation
    b. educational level
    c. religion
    d. recreational lifestyle

44. Currently more than _____ percent of all U.S. preschool children are in day care, either in private homes or institutional settings.
    a. 21
    b. 50
    c. 74
    d. 80

45. _____ theorists stress that socialization contributes to *false consciousness*, which is a lack of awareness and a distorted perception of the reality of social class as it affects all aspects of social life.
    a. Conflict
    b. Functionalist
    c. Symbolic Interactionist
    d. Postmodern

46. Studies have found that day-care and preschool programs have a _____ effect on the overall socialization of children.
    a. positive
    b. neutral
    c. negative
    d. (no studies have been able to address this issue)

47. Sociologists who adopt a conflict perspective suggest that schools _____.
    a. teach students to be productive members of society
    b. transmit culture from one generation to the next
    c. guide students in their personal development
    d. teach a "hidden curriculum"

48. Individuals must earn their acceptance by their peers by conforming to a given group's norms, attitudes, speech patterns, and dress codes. This situation is known as _____.
    a. issues conformity
    b. peer pressure
    c. status inconsistency
    d. peer group process

49. A(n) _____ is a group of people who are linked by common interests, equal social position, and (usually) similar age.
   a. social group
   b. status group
   c. peer group
   d. interaction group

50. _____ provide children with some degree of freedom from parents and other authority figures.
   a. Social groups
   b. Status groups
   c. Peer groups
   d. Interaction groups

51. It is estimated that U.S. children spend _____ hours per day watching television programs.
   a. 1.0
   b. 2.0
   c. 2.5
   d. 4.3

52. Researchers from the Annenberg Public Policy Center found that 93 percent of children between the ages of 10 and 17 know the names of characters on the Fox series *The Simpsons*, but only _____ percent could name the current vice president of the United States.
   a. 13
   b. 42
   c. 63
   d. 82

53. _____ is the aspect of socialization that contains specific messages and practices concerning the nature of being female or male in a specific group or society.
   a. Sex difference
   b. Gender difference
   c. Gender socialization
   d. Sexual learning

54. According to a recent study, about _____ U.S. children spend some time on-line.
   a. 1 million
   b. 10 million
   c. 50 million
   d. 200 million

55. In a poll conducted after the 1999 Columbine (Colorado) High Schools shootings, _____ percent of those surveyed indicated that they believed the Internet and the World Wide Web were at least partly to blame for the shootings.
    a. 23
    b. 38
    c. 61
    d. 82

56. Scholars have found that ethnic values and attitudes begin to crystallize among children as young as age _____.
    a. 6 months
    b. 18 month
    c. 2 years
    d. 4 years

57. Sociologists believe that the socialization process takes place _____.
    a. only during infancy
    b. almost exclusively during childhood
    c. almost exclusively during childhood and adolescence
    d. throughout the lifespan

58. Which of the following groups reinforces traditional gender roles by rigidly dividing events into male and female categories?
    a. peer groups
    b. schools
    c. the media
    d. sports

59. Sociologist Patricia Hill Collins has suggested that the gender socialization of African American children may be deeply influenced by women other than their biological mothers. Collins refers to these women as _____.
    a. othermothers
    b. community mothers
    c. role mothers
    d. mentor mothers

60. _____ is the aspect of socialization that contains specific messages and practices concerning the nature of one's racial or ethnic status.
    a. Total socialization
    b. Ethnic succession
    c. Racial valuing
    d. Racial socialization

61. Social activities based on age or other factors, that publicly dramatize and validate changes in a person's status are referred to as _____.
   a. rites of passage
   b. status change systems
   c. public affirmations
   d. status rituals

62. Some scholars and therapists believe that children who are abused have a greater likelihood of becoming abusive parents themselves. This idea is known as the _____ hypothesis.
   a. intergenerational
   b. genetic
   c. cultural lag
   d. structural generation

63. In industrialized societies, persons in their teenage years must find their own paths to self-identity and adulthood. Another term that scholars use for persons in their teenage years is _____.
   a. bairn
   b. adolescents
   c. early adults
   d. developed children

64. Persons in their teenage years often spend much of their time planning or being educated for future roles they hope to occupy. This process is known as _____.
   a. role conflict
   b. anticipatory socialization
   c. reflective socialization
   d. occupational anticipation

65. A driver's license test, high school graduation day, and a marriage ceremony are examples of _____.
   a. rites of passage
   b. status change systems
   c. status rituals
   d. public affirmations

66. Sociologists refer to persons who are between the ages of _____ as the young-old.
   a. 45-60
   b. 61-64
   c. 65-74
   d. 75-85

67. Sociologists refer to persons who are between the ages of _____ as the *old-old*.
    a. 61-64
    b. 65-74
    c. 75-85
    d. 86-100

68. Which of the following age groups tends to experience the most *social devaluation* in industrialized societies?
    a. children
    b. adolescents
    c. young adults
    d. older adults

69. Industrial Designer Patricia Moore, age 27, disguised herself as an 85-year-old woman. When she went to various locations such as grocery stores, she found that _____.
    a. people would often go out of their way to help her
    b. young men were most likely to give up their place in line to her
    c. checkout clerks sometimes yelled at her
    d. people standing in line often asked her if she was "really" old

70. _____ is the process of learning a new and different set of attitudes, values, and behaviors from those in one's background and previous experience.
    a. Anticipatory socialization
    b. Postmodern socialization
    c. Resocialization
    d. Postsocialization

71. Religious conversion, becoming a student, and retiring from a job are examples of _____.
    a. anticipatory socialization
    b. postmodern socialization
    c. resocialization
    d. postsocialization

72. A(n) _____ is a place where people are isolated from the rest of society for a set period of time and come under the control of the officials who run the institution.
    a. obedience institution
    b. social institution
    c. total institution
    d. conforming institution

73. Military boot camps, prisons, jails, concentration camps, and some mental hospitals are examples of _____.
    a. obedience institutions
    b. social institutions
    c. total institutions
    d. conforming institutions

74. According to sociologist Erving Goffman, people entering places such as prisons and military boot camps are required to undergo a(n) _____ that totally strips them of their former selves.
    a. interaction ritual
    b. booking ceremony
    c. entering rite
    d. degradation ceremony

75. According to your textbook, which of the following social institutions is likely to remain most important in shaping and nurturing personal values and self-identity?
    a. family
    b. education
    c. religion
    d. government

True-False Questions

1. All states require teachers in child-care centers to have training in their field and to pass a licensing examination.

2. The cost of child care is a major financial burden for many U.S. families.

3. Humans differ from nonhuman animals because we lack instincts and must rely on learning for our survival.

4. The cases of Anna and Genie–children raised in relative isolation from human contact– illustrate the fact that children are born with most of the skills that they need in order to survive in human society.

5. The definition of which acts constitute child abuse is the same in nearly every society.

6. Cognitive theorist Jean Piaget proposed that children must master each stage of cognitive development before they can proceed to the next stage.

7. According to Psychologist Carol Gilligan, men and women are socialized to think about moral problems according to different standards.

8. George Herbert Mead divided the self into the "I" and the "Me." The "I" is the objective element of the self, which is composed of the internalized attitudes and demands of others, and the individual's awareness of those demands.

9. According to George Herbert Mead, the "I" develops before the "Me."

10. Sociologists believe that the bulk of the socialization that children experience occurs in school.

11. According to George Herbert Mead, children in the *game stage* of development of the self are able to understand the expectations of others.

12. Recent studies suggest that, by the time students graduate from high school, they will have spent more time in front of the television set than sitting in the classroom.

13. In nearly every culture of the world, parents prefer male children to female children.

14. Working-class families tend to adhere to less-rigid gender expectations than do middle-class families.

15. Resocialization is nearly always a voluntary process.

Chapter 3: Answers to Practice Test Questions

(question-answer-page)

Multiple Choice Questions

1. c 71	41. a 84	6. T 76
2. a 72	42. a 84	7. T 79
3. c 72	43. a 85	8. F 81
4. a 72	44. b 85	9. T 81
5. d 72	45. a 85	10. F 84
6. a 73	46. a 85	11. T 82
7. b 74	47. d 86	12. T 87
8. c 73	48. b 86	13. T 88
9. b 75	49. c 86	14. F 89
10. a 76	50. c 86	15. F 94
11. a 76	51. c 87	
12. d 76	52. c 88	
13. a 76	53. c 88	
14. a 76	54. b 88	
15. a 76	55. d 88	
16. c 76	56. d 89	
17. c 76	57. d 89	
18. a 76	58. d 89	
19. c 77	59. a 89	
20. b 77	60. d 89	
21. d 78	61. a 90	
22. b 78	62. a 91	
23. b 78	63. b 91	
24. c 78	64. b 91	
25. a 78	65. a 92	
26. b 78	66. c 92	
27. b 79	67. c 92	
28. a 79	68. d 93	
29. b 79	69. c 93	
30. c 79	70. c 94	
31. b 80	71. c 94	
32. d 80	72. c 95	
33. c 81	73. c 95	
34. b 81	74. d 95	
35. a 82	75. a 95	
36. c 82		
37. c 83	**True-False Questions**	
38. d 83	1. F 71	
39. b 83	2. T 71	
40. d 84	3. T 73	
	4. F 75	
	5. F 76	

Chapter 4
Social Structure and Interaction in Everyday Life

Multiple Choice Questions

1. Author Lars Eighner spent a period of time as a homeless person, during which he learned to scavenge food and other items from trash containers. Eighner refers to this practice as _____.
    a. dump picking
    b. dumpster diving
    c. Divine Providence
    d. gleaning

2. _____ is the process by which people act toward or respond to other people.
    a. Societal reaction
    b. Socialization
    c. Social interaction
    d. Symbolic socialization

3. _____ is the stable pattern of social relationships that exists within a particular group or society.
    a. Interactional pattern
    b. Social structure
    c. Social status
    d. Resocialization

4. Less than _____ percent of all homeless persons are that way by choice.
    a. 6
    b. 12
    c. 34
    d. 42

5. About _____ percent of homeless persons hold full- or part-time jobs but earn too little to find an affordable place to live.
    a. 6
    b. 12
    c. 20
    d. 35

6. It is inaccurate to say that most homeless persons are mentally ill. In fact, estimates suggest that about _____ percent of homeless persons are mentally ill.
    a. 3
    b. 12
    c. 25
    d. 39

7. According to the _____ perspective, social structure is essential because it creates order and predictability in a society.
    a. functionalist
    b. conflict
    c. symbolic interactionist
    d. postmodern

8. At the macrolevel, the social structure of a society has several essential elements: social institutions, groups, statuses, roles, and _____.
    a. values
    b. norms
    c. races
    d. prestige

9. According to social theorist _____, in capitalist societies, where a few people control the labor of many, the social structure reflects a system of relationships of domination among categories of people.
    a. Karl Marx
    b. Emile Durkheim
    c. Ferdinand Tönnies
    d. Harold Garfinkel

10. _____ is the state of being part insider and part outsider in the social structure.
    a. Borderline status
    b. Social marginality
    c. Stigma
    d. Punishment

11. A _____ is any physical or social attribute or sign that so devalues a person's social identity that it disqualifies that person from full social acceptance.
    a. borderline status
    b. social marginality
    c. stigma
    d. punishment

12. A _____ is a socially defined position in a group or society characterized by certain expectations, rights, and duties.
    a. status
    b. role
    c. label
    d. cohort

13. Statuses differ according to the manner that persons acquire them. A(n) _____ status is a social position conferred at birth or received involuntarily later in life.
    a. master
    b. achieved
    c. ascribed
    d. earned

14. A(n) _____ status is a social position a person assumes voluntarily as a result of personal choice, merit, or direct effort.
    a. master
    b. achieved
    c. ascribed
    d. positive

15. Race/ethnicity, age, and gender are examples of _____ statuses.
    a. master
    b. achieved
    c. ascribed
    d. earned

16. Occupation, education, and income are examples of _____ statuses.
    a. master
    b. achieved
    c. ascribed
    d. positive

17. How many social statuses does one person usually occupy at a time?
    a. one
    b. two
    c. three
    d. many

18. A(n) _____ status is the most important status a person occupies; it dominates all of the individual's other statuses.
    a. master
    b. achieved
    c. ascribed
    d. earned

19. Which of the following statuses has tended to be a master status for men?
    a. religion
    b. age
    c. marital status
    d. occupation

20. Which of the following statuses tends to be a master status for both men and women?
   a. age
   b. homelessness
   c. religious affiliation
   d. physical attractiveness

21. Which of the following statuses has tended to be a master status for women?
   a. housewife
   b. religious affiliation
   c. age
   d. education

22. Wedding rings, expensive automobiles, and fancy clothes are examples of _____.
   a. role expectations
   b. status symbols
   c. status inconsistencies
   d. innate intelligence

23. In a hospital that is attached to a medical school, medical personnel wear uniform coats of different colors and lengths, depending on the job that they do and their position in the hierarchy of social prestige. In this instance, uniform coats are an example of _____.
   a. role expectations
   b. status symbols
   c. negative sanctions
   d. role distance

24. According to Linton, we occupy a _____ and we play a _____.
   a. role, status
   b. status, role
   c. value, norm
   d. norm, value

25. A carpenter who is hired to renovate a kitchen is not expected to sit down uninvited and join the family (employer) for dinner. This illustrates the concept of _____.
   a. status
   b. role
   c. value
   d. norm

26. _____ is a group's or society's definition of the way a specific role ought to be played.
   a. Role expectation
   b. Role performance
   c. Role evaluation
   d. Role script

27. _____ is how a person actually performs a given role.
    a. Role expectation
    b. Role performance
    c. Role evaluation
    d. Role script

28. _____ are typically based on a range of acceptable behavior rather than on strictly defined standards. In other words, definitions of how a role ought to be played can be highly specific or less structured, depending on the status to which the role is attached.
    a. Role expectations
    b. Role performances
    c. Role evaluations
    d. Role scripts

29. _____ attached to the status of surgeon or college professor are highly specific, as opposed to those that are attached to the status of friend.
    a. Role expectations
    b. Role performances
    c. Role evaluations
    d. Role scripts

30. Sometimes the expectations associated with a role are unclear, such as when a child turns 18 and her parents are unsure about whether to continue their provider role. This situation is referred to as _____.
    a. role performance
    b. status inconsistency
    c. role ambiguity
    d. status uncertainty

31. Charles is a college student, his parent's son, his girlfriend's boyfriend, and a worker at the neighborhood convenience store. Sometimes these statuses pressure Charles to do things that are incompatible with each other, like attend class, attend his father's surgery, and go out with his girlfriend (all at the same time). This situation is referred to as _____.
    a. role ambiguity
    b. status uncertainty
    c. role strain
    d. role conflict

32. _____ occurs when incompatible role demands are placed on a person by two or more statuses held at the same time.
    a. Role ambiguity
    b. Status uncertainty
    c. Role strain
    d. Role conflict

33. _____ occurs when incompatible demands are built into a single status.
    a. Role ambiguity
    b. Status uncertainty
    c. Role strain
    d. Role conflict

34. Married women may experience more _____ than married men because of work overload, marital inequality with their spouse, exclusive parenting responsibilities, unclear expectations, and lack of emotional support.
    a. role ambiguity
    b. status uncertainty
    c. role strain
    d. role conflict

35. Lesbians and gay men often experience _____ because of the pressures associated with having an identity heavily stigmatized by the dominant cultural group.
    a. role ambiguity
    b. status uncertainty
    c. role strain
    d. role conflict

36. Mortimer is a 25-year-old single man who enjoys riding the merry-go-round ride by himself at the local amusement park. To avoid embarrassment, Mortimer adopts a bored-looking attitude and body posture while he is on the ride. This is an example of _____.
    a. role distancing
    b. role exit
    c. role ambiguity
    d. role conflict

37. Sometimes people must disengage from social roles that have been central to their self-identity. This process is known as _____.
    a. role distancing
    b. role exit
    c. role ambiguity
    d. role ending

38. Christopher, a former crack addict who had lived in New York City subway stations, was able to become a domiciled person (a person with a home) after completing a drug rehabilitation program. Christopher's experience is an example of _____.
    a. role distancing
    b. role exit
    c. role ambiguity
    d. role ending

39. A _____ consists of two or more people who interact frequently and share a common identity and a feeling of interdependence.
    a. subculture
    b. social group
    c. counterculture
    d. cult

40. A _____ is a small, less specialized group in which members engage in face-to-face, emotion-based interactions over an extended period of time.
    a. primary group
    b. secondary group
    c. tertiary group
    d. formal organization

41. A _____ is a larger more specialized group in which members engage in more impersonal, goal-oriented relationships for a limited period of time.
    a. primary group
    b. secondary group
    c. tertiary group
    d. peer group

42. Families, close friends, and peer groups are examples of _____.
    a. primary groups
    b. secondary groups
    c. tertiary groups
    d. formal organizations

43. Schools, churches, and corporations are examples of _____.
    a. primary groups
    b. secondary groups
    c. tertiary groups
    d. peer groups

44. _____ link people with other people in a web of social relationships.
    a. Role exits
    b. Tertiary groups
    c. Social networks
    d. Total institutions

45. In order to enhance their business contacts, business owners and managers frequently join community groups and organizations such as the Chamber of Commerce, the Lion's Club or the local golf club. This is an example of _____.
    a. primary groups
    b. social networks
    c. total institutions
    d. role strain

46.   A _____ is a highly structured group formed for the purpose of completing certain tasks or achieving specific goals.
       a.   primary group
       b.   self-fulfilling prophecy
       c.   formal organization
       d.   master status

47.   Which of the following terms best describes the situation of homeless persons, according to sociologist Peter Rossi?
       a.   solidarity
       b.   isolation
       c.   role performance
       d.   achieved status

48.   The Salvation Army, women's shelters, and other caregiver organizations provide services to needy groups, but at the same time they must also work with limited monetary resources, and also maintain control over their clientele. This type of organization is referred to by sociologists as a _____.
       a.   people-processing organization
       b.   primary group
       c.   social structure organization
       d.   status symbol conglomerate

49.   A _____ is a set of organized beliefs and rules that establishes how a society will attempt to meet its basic social needs.
       a.   formal organization
       b.   people-processing organization
       c.   social institution
       d.   culture

50.   The family, education, religion, the economy, and government/politics are the five basic _____ in society.
       a.   formal organizations
       b.   people-processing organizations
       c.   social institutions
       d.   cultures

51.   The mass media, sports, science, and medicine are examples of _____.
       a.   formal organizations
       b.   people-processing organizations
       c.   social institutions
       d.   cultures

52. According to the _____ perspective, social institutions perform essential tasks such as replacing members and preserving order, for the benefit of all of society's members.
    a. functionalist
    b. conflict
    c. symbolic interactionist
    d. feminist

53. According to the _____ perspective, all societies must provide and distribute goods and services for their members. The economy is the primary social institution fulfilling this need.
    a. functionalist
    b. conflict
    c. symbolic interactionist
    d. feminist

54. According to the _____ perspective, social institutions such as the government maintain the privileges of the wealthy and powerful while contributing to the powerlessness of others.
    a. functionalist
    b. conflict
    c. symbolic interactionist
    d. postmodern

55. According to early sociologist _____, society is held together by mechanical solidarity or organic solidarity, depending on the type of society.
    a. Ferdinand Tönnies
    b. Emile Durkheim
    c. Max Weber
    d. Karl Marx

56. According to Emile Durkheim, the form of social cohesion that is found in preindustrial societies, in which there is a minimal division of labor, and people feel united by shared values and common social bonds, is _____.
    a. Gemeinschaft
    b. *Gesellschaft*
    c. organic solidarity
    d. mechanical solidarity

57. According to Emile Durkheim, the form of social cohesion that is found in industrial (and perhaps postindustrial) societies, in which people perform very specialized tasks and feel united by their mutual dependence, is _____.
    a. Gemeinschaft
    b. *Gesellschaft*
    c. organic solidarity
    d. mechanical solidarity

58.   Sociologist Ferdinand Tönnies suggested that _____ is a traditional society in which social relationships are based on personal bonds of friendship and kinship and on intergenerational stability.
      a.   the Gemeinschaft
      b.   the *Gesellschaft*
      c.   organic solidarity
      d.   mechanical solidarity

59.   According to Tönnies, _____ is a large, urban society in which social bonds are based on impersonal and specialized relationships, with little long-term commitment to the group or consensus on values.
      a.   the Gemeinschaft
      b.   the *Gesellschaft*
      c.   organic solidarity
      d.   mechanical solidarity

60.   According to Tönnies' typology, the United States would be classified as a(n) _____.
      a.   Gemeinschaft
      b.   *Gesellschaft*
      c.   primary group
      d.   secondary group

61.   Which of the following theoretical perspectives looks at society from a microlevel point of view?
      a.   functionalist theory
      b.   conflict theory
      c.   symbolic interactionist theory
      d.   feminist theory

62.   According to Erving Goffman, strangers meeting each other on the street will look at each other just long enough to acknowledge each others' presence, then they will look away. This is an example of _____.
      a.   the self-fulfilling prophecy
      b.   status inconsistency
      c.   civil disobedience
      d.   civil inattention

63.   According to Berger and Luckmann's idea of _____, our perception of reality is largely shaped by the subjective meaning that we give to an experience. That is, we create our own views of reality in interactions with others.
      a.   functionalist theory
      b.   conflict theory
      c.   the social construction of reality
      d.   reality therapy

64. A _____ is a false belief or prediction that produces behavior that makes the originally false belief come true.
   a. self-fulfilling prophecy
   b. symbolic inaccuracy
   c. social inconsistency
   d. stigma

65. The school of thought known as _____ is the study of the common sense knowledge that people use to understand the situations in which they find themselves.
   a. nonverbal communication
   b. ethnomethodology
   c. sociobiology
   d. feminism

66. Erving Goffman's _____ approach looks at social interaction as if it were a theatrical performance.
   a. ethnomethodological
   b. psychological
   c. historical
   d. dramaturgical

67. People usually attempt to present themselves to others in ways that are most favorable to their own interests or image. Sociologist Erving Goffman refers to this process as _____.
   a. the self-fulfilling prophecy
   b. organic solidarity
   c. role exit
   d. impression management

68. Sociologist Erving Goffman refers to the area where a player performs a specific role before an audience as _____.
   a. back stage
   b. front stage
   c. out front
   d. primary territory

69. Erving Goffman points out that people often help others save face by overlooking or ignoring flaws in their social performances. He refers to this process as _____.
   a. studied nonobservance
   b. social immunity
   c. failure to succeed
   d. social humanity

70. Sociologist Arlie Hochschild suggests that people are often required to display certain emotions to the people they encounter in the course of their work. Flight attendants, for example, are required to act friendly, helpful, and to smile at airline passengers. This display of appropriate emotions in the job context is referred to as _____.
    a. ethnomethodology
    b. the dramaturgical approach
    c. false emotions
    d. emotional labor

71. According to C. Wright Mills, emotional labor may produce _____.
    a. alienation
    b. enhanced status
    c. physical symptoms
    d. anomie

72. The subfield of sociology that deals with how persons express their feelings, and how they conform the expression of feelings to the requirements of social interaction, is called _____.
    a. ethnomethodology
    b. the dramaturgical approach
    c. the sociology of emotions
    d. postmodern sociology

73. Visual cues (gestures, appearances), vocal features (inflection, volume, pitch), and environmental factors (use of space, position) are examples of _____.
    a. nonverbal communication
    b. organic solidarity
    c. role distance
    d. social structure

74. According to Erving Goffman, _____ is the symbolic means by which subordinates give a required permissive response to those in power; it confirms the existence of inequality and reaffirms each person's relationship to the other.
    a. deference
    b. demeanor
    c. nonverbal communication
    d. the self-fulfilling prophecy

75. According to the sociological perspective, homelessness is primarily caused by _____.
    a. laziness on the part of homeless people
    b. mental illness
    c. the need for welfare reform
    d. the social structure

True-False Questions

1. In recent years, families have accounted for more than half of the homeless population.

2. Most homeless persons are heavy drug users.

3. Homelessness has always existed throughout the history of the United States.

4. Race is an example of an achieved status.

5. Education is an example of an achieved status.

6. To sociologists, the term *status* refers to high levels of prestige, and high positions in society.

7. Homelessness is usually a master status.

8. In order for a woman to perform the role of professor, there must be people present to perform the complementary role of students.

9. Most people occupy only a single social status at one time.

10. Female athletes sometimes experience incongruent expectations and pressures associated with being a woman and an athlete. This is an example of *role strain*.

11. Women in their thirties often experience the highest levels of role strain because of the conflicting demands of work and family obligations.

12. Charles is a college student who works part-time at a fast-food restaurant. When his friends come in, he tells them that "I work here but I wouldn't eat here." This is an example of *role exit*.

13. Social networks typically do not work effectively for poor and homeless individuals.

14. According to Emile Durkheim, people in preindustrial societies are united by their shared values and common bonds.

15. According to Emile Durkheim, people in advanced societies are united by their mutual dependence on each other.

Chapter 4: Answers to Practice Test Questions

(question-answer-page)

Multiple Choice Questions

1. b 100
2. c 100
3. b 100
4. a 102
5. c 101
6. c 102
7. a 102
8. b 102
9. a 103
10. b 103
11. c 104
12. a 104
13. c 104
14. b 104
15. c 104
16. b 104
17. d 104
18. a 105
19. d 105
20. b 105
21. a 105
22. b 106
23. b 106
24. b 106
25. b 106
26. a 106
27. b 106
28. a 106
29. a 107
30. c 107
31. d 107
32. d 107
33. c 108
34. c 108
35. c 108
36. a 108
37. b 108
38. b 108
39. b 109
40. a 109

41. b 109
42. a 109
43. b 109
44. c 110
45. b 110
46. c 110
47. b 110
48. a 111
49. c 111
50. c 111
51. c 111
52. a 111
53. a 111
54. b 112
55. b 112
56. d 112
57. c 112
58. a 113
59. b 113
60. b 113
61. c 113
62. d 116
63. c 117
64. a 117
65. b 117
66. d 119
67. d 119
68. b 119
69. a 119
70. d 120
71. a 120
72. c 120
73. a 122
74. a 122
75. d 125

True-False Questions

1. T 101
2. F 102
3. T 102
4. F 103
5. T 103
6. F 104
7. T 105
8. T 106
9. F 107
10. F 107
11. T 108
12. F 108
13. T 110
14. T 112
15. T 112

Chapter 5
Groups and Organizations

Multiple Choice Questions

1. Research suggests that between 42 and _____ percent of working women have been sexually harassed at some time during the course of their careers.
    a. 48
    b. 68
    c. 88
    d. 98

2. A(n) _____ is a collection of people who happen to be in the same place at the same time but share little else in common.
    a. group
    b. aggregate
    c. cohort
    d. category

3. A _____ is made up of people who may never have met one another but share a similar characteristic such as educational level or race.
    a. group
    b. aggregate
    c. cohort
    d. category

4. Which of the following is an example of a *category*?
    a. first-year graduate students
    b. several people waiting for a traffic light to change
    c. shoppers in a department store
    d. passengers on an airplane flight

5. Which of the following represents an *aggregate*?
    a. shoppers in a department store
    b. Native Americans
    c. women
    d. victims of sexual harassment

6. According to Charles Horton Cooley, a _____ is a small, less specialized group in which members engage in face-to-face, emotion-based interactions over an extended period of time.
    a. primary group
    b. secondary group
    c. formal organization
    d. reference group

7. Formal organizations are _____.
    a. primary groups
    b. secondary groups
    c. significant others
    d. reference groups

8. According to Charles Horton Cooley, a _____ is a larger, more specialized group in which the members engage in more impersonal, goal-oriented relationships for a limited period of time.
    a. primary group
    b. secondary group
    c. peer group
    d. reference group

9. We have primary relationships with other individuals in our primary groups–that is, our _____, who frequently serve as role models.
    a. group cohorts
    b. age peers
    c. significant others
    d. outgroup others

10. According to William Graham Sumner, a(n) _____ is a group to which a person belongs and with which the person feels a sense of identity.
    a. ingroup
    b. outgroup
    c. home group
    d. identity group

11. According to William Graham Sumner, a(n) _____ is a group to which a person does not belong and toward which the person may feel a sense of competitiveness or hostility.
    a. ingroup
    b. outgroup
    c. reference group
    d. peer group

12. Ingroup members often feel that they are superior to persons outside their group. This is known as _____.
    a. identity coherence
    b. false consciousness
    c. ethnomethodology
    d. ethnocentrism

13. When people attempt to evaluate their appearance, ideas, or goals, they automatically refer to the standards of some group, which sociologists call their _____ .
    a. outgroup
    b. cohort
    c. reference group
    d. secondary group

14. According to the _____ perspective, people form groups to meet instrumental and expressive needs.
    a. functionalist
    b. conflict
    c. symbolic interactionist
    d. postmodern

15. Instrumental needs are _____ .
    a. related to emotions
    b. task-oriented
    c. unnecessary
    d. impossible to meet

16. Expressive needs are _____ .
    a. related to emotions
    b. task-oriented
    c. unnecessary
    d. impossible to meet

17. According to the _____ perspective, groups meet needs, but they also involve a series of power relationships that benefit some persons and not others.
    a. functionalist
    b. conflict
    c. symbolic interactionist
    d. postmodern

18. According to the postmodern perspective, groups are _____ .
    a. too large
    b. superficial
    c. cohesive
    d. too complex

19. _____ focus on how the size of a group influences the kind of interaction that takes place among members.
    a. Functionalists
    b. Conflict theorists
    c. Symbolic Interactionists
    d. Postmodern theorists

20. The smallest number of people that are necessary to form a social group is _____ .
    a. one
    b. two
    c. three
    d. five

21. A dyad is a group that is composed of _____ members.
    a. one
    b. two
    c. three
    d. five

22. According to Georg Simmel, each of the members of a _____ has the power to withdraw, and cause the group to cease to exist.
    a. dyad
    b. triad
    c. primary group
    d. secondary group

23. Two people who are best friends, married couples, and domestic partners are examples of _____ .
    a. dyads
    b. triads
    c. reference groups
    d. secondary groups

24. People sometimes accept the values and norms of a group with which we identify rather than one to which we belong. We may also act more like members of a group we want to join than the members of groups to which we already belong. In these cases, reference groups are a source of _____ .
    a. instrumental leadership
    b. rationality
    c. anticipatory socialization
    d. expressive leadership

25. As compared with small groups, large groups typically have _____ solidarity.
    a. less
    b. about the same amount of
    c. more
    d. (there is no way to tell)

26. One of the key determinants of a group's power is its _____, which is defined as the number of potential members that the group has.
    a. absolute size
    b. relative size
    c. potential width
    d. extrapolated membership

27. Groups have various leadership styles. _____ leaders make all major group decisions and assign tasks to members.
    a. Authoritarian
    b. Participatory
    c. Laissez-faire
    d. Democratic

28. Groups have various leadership styles. _____ leaders are only minimally involved in decision making and encourage group members to make their own decisions.
    a. Authoritarian
    b. Democratic
    c. Laissez-faire
    d. Autocratic

29. _____ group leaders encourage group discussion and decision making through consensus building.
    a. Authoritarian
    b. Democratic
    c. Laissez-faire
    d. Autocratic

30. Groups require _____ of their members, which is the process of maintaining or changing behavior to comply with the norms established by the group.
    a. solidarity
    b. values
    c. evolution
    d. conformity

31. Solomon Asch conducted a series of experiments in which a subject compared a series of lines with six other "subjects" who where actually part of the experiment. Asch found that _____.
    a. subjects are influenced by group pressure to conform
    b. subjects are able to resist group pressure to conform
    c. the study was invalid, since the lines were not the same length
    d. research subjects rarely lie

32. _____ is a form of compliance in which people follow direct orders from someone in a position of authority.
    a.   resistance
    b.   role exit
    c.   evolution
    d.   obedience

33. Stanley Milgram's teacher/learner experiment examined the extent to which research subjects would _____.
    a.   follow the instructions of an authority figure
    b.   be able to withstand electrical shock
    c.   correctly identify numerous species of birds
    d.   be able to function after drinking various amounts of alcohol

34. In Stanley Milgram's teacher/learner experiment, all research subjects were told that they were free to leave at any time. Why did they stay and continue with the experiment?
    a.   because the teacher told them to continue
    b.   because they knew they would not be paid if they left early
    c.   because they believed that the experiment was ethical and reasonable
    d.   because they knew that the "learners" were not receiving real electric shocks

35. _____ is the process by which members of a cohesive group arrive at a decision that many individual members privately believe is unwise.
    a.   Collective incoherence
    b.   Groupthink
    c.   Group false consciousness
    d.   Committee inaccuracy

36. The decision-making process among officials of NASA and the companies responsible for designing and manufacturing the space shuttle *Challenger*, which exploded soon after launch in 1986, exhibits the concept of _____.
    a.   collective incoherence
    b.   groupthink
    c.   group false consciousness
    d.   committee inaccuracy

37. The number of formal organizations has _____ in the United States over the past century.
    a.   sharply decreased
    b.   slightly decreased
    c.   remained about the same
    d.   increased sharply

38. Which of the following is an example of *formal organizations*?
    a. corporations
    b. schools
    c. government agencies
    d. (all of the above)

39. Formal organizations are formed for the purpose of _____.
    a. conforming to government regulations
    b. efficiently achieving specific goals
    c. reducing the tax burden of corporations
    d. meeting their members' emotional needs

40. According to sociologist Amitai Etzioni, we join _____ organizations when we want to pursue some common interest or gain personal satisfaction or prestige from being a member.
    a. utilitarian
    b. coercive
    c. normative
    d. bureaucratic

41. According to sociologist Amitai Etzioni, _____ organizations are associations that people are forced to join.
    a. utilitarian
    b. coercive
    c. normative
    d. bureaucratic

42. According to sociologist Amitai Etzioni, people join _____ organizations when they can provide us with a material reward that we seek.
    a. utilitarian
    b. coercive
    c. normative
    d. bureaucratic

43. The most universal organizational form in government, business, education, and religion is the _____ organization.
    a. utilitarian
    b. coercive
    c. normative
    d. bureaucratic

44. A _____ organization is characterized by a hierarchy of authority, a clear division of labor, explicit rules and procedures, and impersonality in personnel matters.
    a. utilitarian
    b. coercive
    c. normative
    d. bureaucratic

45. Bureaucracies sometimes seem to foster the situation in which there is so much paperwork and so many incomprehensible rules that no one really understands what to do. This situation has been refered to as _____.
    a. paralysis
    b. "red tape"
    c. pink-collar occupations
    d. "rule obsession"

46. Which of the following groups or organizations is likely to have a bureaucratic structure?
    a. a college
    b. a small family grocery store
    c. a group of close friends
    d. a rock-and-roll band

47. According to Max Weber, _____ is the process by which traditional methods of social organization, characterized by informality and spontaneity, are gradually replaced by efficiently administered formal rules and procedures.
    a. rationality
    b. urbanization
    c. demography
    d. conformity

48. Max Weber often relied on a(n) _____ analysis, which is an abstract model that describes the recurring characteristics of some phenomenon.
    a. stereotypical
    b. ideal-type
    c. fuzzy logic
    d. hierarchy

49. In order to describe what a typical bureaucracy is like, Max Weber used the method of
    _____.
    a. ideal-types
    b. stereotypes
    c. exemplars
    d. archetypes

50. Weber's model of bureaucracy emphasizes the efficiency and productivity of these types of organizations. However, Weber has been criticized for _____.
   a. not placing enough emphasis on hierarchy and authority
   b. ignoring the fact that each member of a bureaucracy performs a specific task
   c. placing too much emphasis on favoritism and family connections in bureaucratic hiring
   d. ignoring informal networks in bureaucratic organizations

51. According to Weber, authority and accountability in a bureaucratic organization are established by _____.
   a. religious principles
   b. rules and regulations
   c. political pressures
   d. informal and personal ties between employees

52. According to Weber, employees in bureaucratic organizations are expected to act toward clients with _____.
   a. arrogance
   b. emotion
   c. impersonality
   d. personal feelings

53. Sociologist George Ritzer suggests that fast-food restaurants and franchise businesses such as Sir Speedy and Jiffy Lube exhibit the four dimensions of formal rationality. Ritzer refers to the emphasis on formal rationality in businesses such as these as the _____ of society.
   a. standardization
   b. McDonaldization
   c. speedup
   d. uniformity processing

54. Which of the following is NOT one of the four dimensions of formal rationality discussed by sociologist George Ritzer?
   a. efficiency
   b. unpredictability
   c. emphasis on quantity rather than quality
   d. control through nonhuman technologies

55. An organization's _____ is composed of those aspects of participants' day-to-day activities and interactions that ignore, bypass, or do not correspond with the official rules and procedures of the bureaucracy.
   a. organization chart
   b. formal structure
   c. informal structure
   d. internal consistency

56. In most organizations there is an informal network of communication between employees that spreads information much faster than do official channels of communication, which tend to be slow and unresponsive. This informal channel of communication is often referred to as the _____.
   a. break room telegraph
   b. grapevine
   c. back channel wireless
   d. email express

57. _____ occurs when the rules in a bureaucratic organization become an end in themselves rather than a means to an end, and organizational survival becomes more important than achievement of goals.
   a. Goal displacement
   b. Red tape
   c. Increased employee morale
   d. Financial uncertainty

58. Sociologist Thorstein Veblen used the term _____ to characterize situations in which workers have become so highly specialized, or have been given such fragmented jobs to do, that they are unable to come up with creative solutions to problems.
   a. division of labor
   b. trained creativity
   c. trained incapacity
   d. learned innovation

59. Sociologist Robert Merton described workers who are more concerned with following correct procedures than they are with getting the job done correctly. He used the term _____ to refer to these workers.
   a. burnout
   b. bureaucratic personality
   c. organization Man
   d. co-opted workers

60. According to sociologist William H. Whyte, Jr., some workers lose their identity apart from the organization for which they work. Whyte used the term _____ to refer to an individual whose life is controlled by the corporation.
   a. burnout
   b. bureaucratic personality
   c. organization Man
   d. co-opted workers

61. According to your textbook, one problem with bureaucratic organizations is that they tend to promote people until they ultimately reach a level where they _____.
    a. are incompetent
    b. are able to exercise authority too well
    c. make more money than the corporation can afford to pay them
    d. do their job so well that their position is eliminated

62. The _____ theory suggests that employment perpetuates social class differences among people. It suggests that middle-class and upper-middle-class employees work in relatively secure and high-paying jobs while poor and working-class employees often work in jobs characterized by low job security, low pay, and few opportunities for promotion.
    a. bifurcated market
    b. oligarchy
    c. gender inequalities
    d. dual labor market

63. According to sociologist Rosabeth Moss Kanter, when white women and people of color work in bureaucratic organizations and they are underrepresented in those organizations, they tend to _____.
    a. feel isolated
    b. be promoted faster than other employees
    c. become victimizers
    d. have more access to mentors than other employees

64. According to sociologist Rosabeth Moss Kanter, bureacratic organizations often tend to _____.
    a. perpetuate gender inequalities
    b. be owned and managed by people of color
    c. be dominated by women
    d. go out of existence relatively quickly

65. Many women employees of bureaucratic organizations do not report incidents of sexual harassment because they _____.
    a. do not think that sexual harassment is wrong
    b. know that sexual harassment is not illegal
    c. fear retribution by superiors and coworkers
    d. know that few organizations have sexual harassment policies

66. In a recent report, the U.S. Army concluded that sexual harassment _____.
    a. does not exist in the Army
    b. exists only in the Army's lower ranks
    c. exists only in the Army's higher ranks
    d. exists throughout the Army

67. Sociologist Max Weber was not completely favorable toward bureaucracies. He believed that such organizations stifle human initiative and creativity, thus producing what he referred to as a(n) _____.
    a.   "corporate prison"
    b.   "iron cage"
    c.   "velvet hammer"
    d.   "workers' leash"

68. Sometimes bureaucracies place an enormous amount of unregulated power in the hands of a very few leaders. This situation is known as a(n) _____.
    a.   representative democracy
    b.   oligarchy
    c.   triad
    d.   bureaucratic type

69. According to German political sociologist Robert Michels, all organizations tend to become bureaucracies ruled by few, who wield power but also have an interest in retaining their power. Michel's observation has become known as _____.
    a.   the iron law of dictatorship
    b.   the bureaucratic nightmare
    c.   the iron law of oligarchy
    d.   corporate condensation

70. In the early 1980s, a movement arose in the United States to *humanize bureaucracy*. Which of the following is NOT a characteristic of more-humane bureaucracies?
    a.   less-rigid hierarchical structures
    b.   greater sharing of power among employees
    c.   helping people meet outside family responsibilities
    d.   more emphasis on traditional approaches to problem-solving

71. The Japanese economy has been extremely productive since World War II. Which of the following is NOT one of the characteristics of Japanese corporations?
    a.   lifetime employment for workers
    b.   managers who become highly specialized about one aspect of the corporation
    c.   quality circles
    d.   encouragement of worker loyalty to the corporation

72. Some sociologists suggest that the Japanese model of group loyalty may not work in the United States because of the U.S. cultural value of _____.
    a.   educational attainment
    b.   monetary success
    c.   individualism
    d.   hard work

73.	Several alternatives to the bureaucratic model have been suggested by analysts. One, the _____ model, calls for the elimination of hierarchy and the boundaries between functions and departments.
	a.	anti-bureaucracy
	b.	vertical
	c.	horizontal
	d.	displacement

74.	The _____ model calls for performance to be measured by customer satisfaction, not profits.
	a.	anti-bureaucracy
	b.	vertical
	c.	horizontal
	d.	displacement

75.	The traditional organizational structure resembles a pyramid-shaped stack of boxes connected by lines. Organizations structured along the lines of the horizontal model will more closely resemble which of the following?
	a.	a pepperoni pizza
	b.	a shamrock
	c.	an inverted pyramid
	d.	(all of the above)

True-False Questions

1.	Primary groups set boundaries by distinguishing between insiders who are members and outsiders who are not, while secondary groups do not set such boundaries.

2.	Formal organizations are secondary groups, but they contain primary groups within them.

3.	Groups boundaries may be formal or informal.

4.	Reference groups (groups to which we might wish to belong) are always positive, never negative.

5.	Sociologists have found that the presence of a common enemy tends to cause two groups to grow apart even further than they already are.

6.	A person's reference group attachments tend to change when he or she acquires a new status in a formal organization.

7.	Large groups typically have more solidarity than small ones.

8.	Large groups typically have more formalized leadership structures than small ones.

9.	The term *compliance* may be defined as the extent to which people do or say things because they have a strong individual belief that these actions are the right thing to do.

10.	In Stanley Milgram's study of obedience, almost two-thirds of the research subjects administered what they thought could be a deadly electric shock to the "learners."

11.	Stanley Milgram's teacher/learner experiment would be considered unethical today, and would not be allowed by colleges and universities.

12.	Men are more likely to become members of normative organizations than women are.

13.	According to sociologist Max Weber, bureaucracies are *rational*.

14.	According to Blau and Meyer, large organizations would be unable to function without strong informal norms and relations among participants.

15.	Men typically fare much better than women in Japanese corporations because patriarchy excludes many women from career-track positions.

Chapter 5: Answers to Practice Test Questions

(question-answer-page)

Multiple Choice Questions

1. c 131
2. b 133
3. d 133
4. a 133
5. a 133
6. a 133
7. b 133
8. b 133
9. c 133
10. a 134
11. b 134
12. d 134
13. c 134
14. a 135
15. b 135
16. a 135
17. b 135
18. b 135
19. c 135
20. b 135
21. b 135
22. a 135
23. a 135
24. c 135
25. a 136
26. b 136
27. a 137
28. c 138
29. b 137
30. d 138
31. a 138
32. d 139
33. a 139
34. a 140
35. b 141
36. b 141
37. d 141
38. d 142
39. b 142
40. c 143

41. b 144
42. a 144
43. d 144
44. d 144
45. b 144
46. a 145
47. a 144
48. b 144
49. a 145
50. d 145
51. b 146
52. c 146
53. b 146
54. b 146
55. c 146
56. b 146
57. a 149
58. c 149
59. b 149
60. c 150
61. a 151
62. d 152
63. a 152
64. a 152
65. c 153
66. d 152
67. b 153
68. b 153
69. c 153
70. d 154
71. b 154
72. c 155
73. c 155
74. c 155
75. d 156

True-False Questions

1. F 133
2. T 133
3. T 134
4. F 135
5. F 135

6. T 135
7. F 136
8. T 136
9. F 139
10. T 140
11. T 140
12. F 143
13. T 144
14. T 147
15. T 155

Chapter 6
Deviance and Crime

Multiple Choice Questions

1. _____ are friendship circles whose members identify one another as mutually connected. According to Patricia Adler and Peter Adler, they "have a hierarchical structure, being dominated by leaders, and are exclusive in nature, so that not all individuals who desire membership are accepted."
   a.   Voluntary organizations
   b.   Cliques
   c.   Differential associations
   d.   Networks

2. A _____ is a group of people, usually young, who band together for purposes generally considered to be deviant or criminal by the larger society.
   a.   clique
   b.   network
   c.   posse
   d.   gang

3. Sociologists define _____ as any behavior, belief, or condition that violates significant social norms in the society or group in which it occurs.
   a.   deviance
   b.   conformity
   c.   crime
   d.   misbehavior

4. Which of the following has been seen as deviant at some time in the United States?
   a.   AIDS
   b.   obesity
   c.   Satanism
   d.   (all of the above)

5. Persons who are viewed as deviant often experience _____, which is any physical or social attribute or sign that so devalues a person's social identity that it disqualifies the person from full social acceptance.
   a.   disability
   b.   stigma
   c.   discrimination
   d.   ethnocentrism

6.   According to sociologists, deviance is _____.
     a.   an inherent property of certain acts
     b.   an inherent property of certain beliefs
     c.   an inherent property of certain conditions
     d.   a social definition by a certain audience

7.   Definitions of deviance vary _____.
     a.   from time to time
     b.   from place to place
     c.   from group to group
     d.   (all of the above)

8.   Keeping a library book past its due date or cutting a class are examples of violation of _____?
     a.   folkways
     b.   mores
     c.   taboos
     d.   laws

9.   Falsifying a college application or cheating on an examination are examples of violations of _____.
     a.   folkways
     b.   mores
     c.   taboos
     d.   informal expectations

10. A _____ is a behavior that violates criminal law and is punishable with fines, jail terms, and/or other negative sanctions.
     a.   folkway
     b.   more
     c.   crime
     d.   transgression

11. _____ refers to a violation of law or the commission of a status offense by young people.
     a.   Crime
     b.   Juvenile Delinquency
     c.   Youthful offenses
     d.   "Wild oats"

12. Behaviors that are illegal only when committed by younger people (such as cutting school or running away from home) are referred to as _____.
     a.   crimes
     b.   youthful behaviors
     c.   reformatory offenses
     d.   status offenses

13. _____ refers to the systematic practices that social groups develop in order to encourage conformity to norms, rules, and laws and to discourage deviance.
    a. Deviance
    b. Juvenile justice
    c. Folkways
    d. Social control

14. _____ involve(s) the use of negative sanctions that proscribe certain behaviors and set forth the punishments for rule breakers and nonconformists.
    a. Internal social control
    b. External social control
    c. Informal sanctions
    d. Social norms

15. In contemporary societies, the criminal justice system, which includes the police, the courts, and the prisons, is the primary mechanism of _____.
    a. internal social control
    b. external social control
    c. informal sanctions
    d. social norms

16. _____ is the systematic study of crime and the criminal justice system, including the police, courts, and prisons.
    a. Sociology of deviance
    b. Criminology
    c. Juvenile delinquency
    d. Sociology of law

17. According to the _____ theoretical perspective, a certain amount of deviance contributes to the smooth functioning of society.
    a. conflict
    b. symbolic interactionist
    c. functionalist
    d. postmodern

18. According to Emile Durkheim, rapid social change may contribute to _____, a social condition in which people experience a sense of futility because social norms are weak, absent, or conflicting.
    a. disability
    b. social solidarity
    c. depression
    d. anomie

19. Which of the following is a function of deviance, as discussed in the textbook?
    a. clarification of rules
    b. unification of groups
    c. promotion of social change
    d. (all of the above are functions of deviance)

20. If too many people violate social norms, then everyday existence may become unpredictable, chaotic, and even violent. In this case, functionalist theorists view deviance as _____.
    a. functional
    b. normal
    c. dysfunctional
    d. inevitable

21. According to Robert Merton, people feel _____ when they are exposed to cultural goals that they are unable to obtain because they do not have access to culturally approved means of achieving those goals.
    a. dysfunctions
    b. functions
    c. depression
    d. strain

22. Functionalist Robert Merton identified five means by which people adapt to cultural goals and approved ways of achieving them. _____ occurs when people abandon both the approved goals and the approved means of achieving them.
    a. Conformity
    b. Innovation
    c. Ritualism
    d. Retreatism

23. Functionalist Robert Merton identified five means by which people adapt to cultural goals and approved ways of achieving them. _____ occurs when people give up on societal goals but still adhere to the socially approved means for achieving them.
    a. Rebellion
    b. Innovation
    c. Ritualism
    d. Retreatism

24. Functionalist Robert Merton identified five means by which people adapt to cultural goals and approved ways of achieving them. _____ occurs when people accept society's goals but adopt disapproved means for achieving them.
    a. Rebellion
    b. Innovation
    c. Ritualism
    d. Retreatism

25. Functionalist Robert Merton identified five means by which people adapt to cultural goals and approved ways of achieving them. _____ occurs when people challenge both the approved goals and the approved means for achieving them and advocate an alternative set of goals or means.
   a. Rebellion
   b. Innovation
   c. Ritualism
   d. Retreatism

26. Functionalist Robert Merton identified five means by which people adapt to cultural goals and approved ways of achieving them. _____ occurs when people accept culturally approved goals and pursue them through approved means.
   a. Conformity
   b. Innovation
   c. Ritualism
   d. Rebellion

27. Sociologists Richard Cloward and Lloyd Ohlin suggest that for deviance to occur, people must have access to _____, which are circumstances that provide an opportunity for people to acquire through illegitimate activities what they cannot achieve through legitimate channels.
   a. illegitimate associates
   b. restricted opportunity structures
   c. illegitimate opportunity structures
   d. restricted social networks

28. Richard Cloward and Lloyd Ohlin identified three basic gang types. The _____ gang is devoted to theft, extortion, and other illegal means of securing an income.
   a. retreatist
   b. conflict
   c. criminal
   d. (none of the above)

29. Richard Cloward and Lloyd Ohlin identified three basic gang types. Members of _____ gangs seek to acquire a reputation by fighting over territory and adopting a value system of toughness, courage, and similar qualities.
   a. retreatist
   b. conflict
   c. criminal
   d. (none of the above)

30. Richard Cloward and Lloyd Ohlin identified three basic gang types. Members of _____ gangs are unable to gain success through legitimate means and are unwilling to do so through illegal ones. As a result, the consumption of drugs is stressed and addiction is prevalent.
    a. retreatist
    b. conflict
    c. criminal
    d. (none of the above)

31. Edwin Sutherland's _____ theory states that people have a greater tendency to deviate from societal norms when they frequently associate with individuals who are more favorable toward deviance than conformity.
    a. Differential Opportunity
    b. Differential Association
    c. Strain
    d. Anomie

32. According to Differential Association theory, deviant behavior is _____.
    a. learned within groups
    b. a result of society's labeling of people as deviant
    c. a result of too few ties to the community
    d. learned from prisoners

33. Social Bond theory suggests that the probability of deviant behavior increases when a person's ties to society are _____.
    a. weakened or broken
    b. strengthened
    c. the result of family connections
    d. (all of the above)

34. _____ states that deviance is a socially constructed process in which social control agencies designate certain people as deviants, and they, in turn, come to accept the label placed upon them and begin to act accordingly.
    a. Strain theory
    b. Anomie theory
    c. Social Bond theory
    d. Labeling theory

35. In William Chambliss' study of the Saints and the Roughnecks, both groups engaged in similar behavior, but the Saints _____.
    a. were more likely to be labeled as deviants
    b. were less likely to be labeled as deviants
    c. came from poorer families
    d. did poorly in school

36. According to Labeling theory, _____ occurs when a person who has been labeled a deviant accepts that new identity and continues the deviant behavior.
    a.   primary deviance
    b.   secondary deviance
    c.   deterrence
    d.   social control

37. According to Labeling theory, _____ is the initial act of rule breaking.
    a.   primary deviance
    b.   secondary deviance
    c.   delinquency
    d.   social control

38. _____ theorists emphasize the importance of differences between people (in terms of power, race, social class, and gender) in determining how laws are created and enforced.
    a.   Conflict
    b.   Functionalist
    c.   Symbolic Interactionist
    d.   Differential Association

39. The branch of Conflict theory known as _____ views deviance and crime as a function of the capitalist economic system.
    a.   Power theory
    b.   Marxist/critical theory
    c.   Labeling theory
    d.   Economic theory

40. According to _____, powerful persons and groups use the criminal law to protect their own interests by controlling those who are without power.
    a.   Power theory
    b.   Marxist/critical theory
    c.   Labeling theory
    d.   Economic theory

41. According to the _____ approach, women's deviance and crime are a rational response to the gender discrimination that women experience in families and the workplace.
    a.   radical feminist
    b.   liberal feminist
    c.   Marxist (socialist) feminist
    d.   (none of the above)

42.   According to the _____ approach, the cause of womens' crime originates in patriarchy (male domination over females).
       a.   radical feminist
       b.   liberal feminist
       c.   Marxist (socialist) feminist
       d.   (none of the above)

43.   According to the _____ approach, women are exploited by both capitalism and patriarchy. For example, because most females have relatively low-wage jobs (if any) and few economic resources, crimes such as prostitution and shoplifting become a means to earn money or acquire consumer goods.
       a.   radical feminist
       b.   liberal feminist
       c.   Marxist (socialist) feminist
       d.   (none of the above)

44.   According to your textbook, Michel Foucault's work in his book entitled *Discipline and Punish* may accurately be classified as an example of _____ theory.
       a.   conflict
       b.   functionalist
       c.   symbolic interactionist
       d.   postmodern

45.   In his book *Discipline and Punish*, Michel Foucault describes a _____, which is a structure that gives prison officials the possibility of complete observation of criminals at all times. For example, a prison might be built which incorporates a tower in the center of a circular prison from which guards can see all the cells.
       a.   cyclotron
       b.   panopticon
       c.   wheel-and-spoke prison
       d.   total observation institution

46.   According to legal definitions, crimes consist of two types, depending on the seriousness of the offense. A _____ is a minor crime that is typically punished by less than one year in jail.
       a.   misdemeanor
       b.   felony
       c.   tort
       d.   capital offense

47.   According to legal definitions, crimes consist of two types, depending on the seriousness of the offense. A _____ is a serious crime such as rape, homicide, or aggravated assault, for which punishment typically ranges from a year's imprisonment to death.
        a.   misdemeanor
        b.   felony
        c.   tort
        d.   violation

48.   Which public body or official determines whether a crime is classified as minor or serious, and what the range of punishments for the offense shall consist of?
        a.   the sheriff
        b.   local police officials
        c.   the prosecutor
        d.   the legislature

49.   The _____ is the main source of information on crimes reported in the United States. It has been compiled since 1930 by the Federal Bureau of Investigation.
        a.   the National Crime Victimization Survey
        b.   the offender self-reports survey
        c.   the Gallup Poll
        d.   the Uniform Crime Reports

50.   _____ focuses on eight major crimes, known as *index crimes*.
        a.   The National Crime Victimization Survey
        b.   The Offender Self-Reports survey
        c.   The Gallup Poll
        d.   The Uniform Crime Reports

51.   Which of the following is NOT an *index crime*?
        a.   murder
        b.   rape
        c.   robbery
        d.   drug sales

52.   Robbery, burglary, larceny, motor vehicle theft, and arson are classified as _____.
        a.   violent crimes
        b.   property crimes
        c.   occupational crimes
        d.   organized crime

53.   Which of the following offenses has been characterized as a "victimless crime" because it involves a willing exchange of services among adults?
        a.   prostitution
        b.   illegal gambling
        c.   illegal pornography
        d.   (all of the above)

54. _____ refers to illegal acts committed by corporate employees on behalf of the corporation and with its support.
   a.   Violent crime
   b.   Organized crime
   c.   Occupational crime
   d.   Corporate crime

55. _____ is made up of illegal activities committed by people in the course of their employment or financial affairs.
   a.   Violent crime
   b.   Organized crime
   c.   Occupational crime
   d.   Corporate crime

56. Antitrust violations, misrepresentations in advertising, price fixing, and financial fraud are examples of _____.
   a.   violent crime
   b.   organized crime
   c.   occupational crime
   d.   corporate crime

57. Drug trafficking, loan-sharking, money laundering, and large-scale theft such as truck hijackings are examples of _____.
   a.   violent crime
   b.   organized crime
   c.   occupational crime
   d.   corporate crime

58. _____ refers to illegal or unethical acts involving the usurpation of power by government officials, or illegal/unethical acts perpetrated against the government by outsiders seeking to make a political statement, undermine the government, or overthrow it.
   a.   Violent crime
   b.   Organized crime
   c.   Political crime
   d.   Terrorism

59. According to the most recent victimization survey, _____ percent of all crimes are not reported to the police and thus are not reflected in the UCR.
   a.   22
   b.   42
   c.   62
   d.   82

60. The Uniform Crime Reports accurately measures _____.
    a. the amount of crime that is committed each year
    b. the amount of crime that is reported each year
    c. (both of the above)
    d. (none of the above)

61. In 1999, men accounted for almost _____ percent of robberies and murders.
    a. 30
    b. 50
    c. 70
    d. 90

62. The peak age category for arrests for index crimes is _____.
    a. 14-15
    b. 16-17
    c. 18-19
    d. 20-21

63. In 1999, African Americans made up about 12 percent of the U.S. population but accounted for about _____ percent of all arrests.
    a. 19
    b. 29
    c. 39
    d. 59

64. Women account for less than _____ percent of all police officers.
    a. 1
    b. 10
    c. 25
    d. 40

65. About _____ percent of criminal cases are never tried in court; instead they are resolved by plea bargaining.
    a. 30
    b. 50
    c. 70
    d. 90

66. _____ is any action designed to deprive a person of things of value (including liberty) because of some offense the person is thought to have committed.
    a. Punishment
    b. Justice
    c. Retribution
    d. Deterrence

67. Punishment may serve four functions. _____ is based on the premise that the more serious the crime, the more serious should be the punishment.
    a. Deterrence
    b. Rehabilitation
    c. Social protection
    d. Retribution

68. Punishment may serve four functions. _____ seeks to reduce criminal activity by instilling a fear of punishment.
    a. Deterrence
    b. Rehabilitation
    c. Social protection
    d. Retribution

69. Punishment may serve four functions. _____ seeks to return offenders to the community as law-abiding citizens.
    a. Deterrence
    b. Rehabilitation
    c. Social protection
    d. Retribution

70. Punishment may serve four functions. _____ results from restricting offenders so that they cannot commit further crimes while they are incarcerated.
    a. Deterrence
    b. Rehabilitation
    c. Social protection
    d. Retribution

71. According to the U.S. Department of Justice, the incarceration rate for African American men in 1996 was _____ the rate for white men.
    a. one half
    b. two times
    c. eight times
    d. twenty times

72. In the 1972 case of *Furman v. Georgia*, the Supreme Court ruled that the death penalty _____.
    a. is cruel and unusual punishment
    b. violates the Eighth Amendment if it is administered arbitrarily
    c. is unconstitutional in all instances
    d. is racially biased, and therefore unconstitutional

73. African Americans are _____ as likely to be sentenced to death for homicidal rape than are whites.
   a. twice
   b. 8-10 times
   c. 15-20 times
   d. 20-30 times

74. Some sociologists suggest that _____--such as more and better education and jobs, affordable housing, more equality and less discrimination--are needed to reduce street crime.
   a. individualized treatment programs
   b. programs that support traditional moral values
   c. structural solutions
   d. urban solutions

75. One of the most pressing crime-related problems in the world today is _____, which is the networking of powerful criminal organizations and their associates in shared activities around the world.
   a. white collar crime
   b. Internet crime
   c. street crime
   d. global crime

True-False Questions

1. Persons may be regarded as deviant if they express a radical or unusual belief system.

2. Individuals who are seen as deviant by one category of people may be seen as conformists by another group.

3. Deviance refers to attitudes and beliefs, but not to specific conditions or characteristics that persons possess.

4. According to sociologists, no act is inherently deviant.

5. According to Emile Durkheim, deviance serves positive social functions.

6. Edwin Sutherland's Differential Association theory suggests that deviance is learned within intimate personal groups.

7. According to feminist theorists, theories developed to explain the behavior of males can also be used to explain female deviance and crime.

8. There is no single feminist perspective on deviance and crime. Instead, several schools of thought have emerged within the feminist theoretical tradition.

9. Most studies of violent crime have included women as subjects or respondents.

10. Criminologists classify robbery as both a violent crime and a property crime.

11. Criminologists classify certain crimes as *street crimes* because all such offenses occur in the street.

12. Most victims of murder are killed by someone who is unknown to them (a stranger).

13. Rates of arrest are higher for males than females at every age and for nearly all offenses.

14. According to your textbook, official crime statistics underreport the actual amount of crime.

15. Womens' prisons generally offer far more educational and training programs than do mens' prisons.

Chapter 6: Answers to Practice Test Questions

(question-answer-page)

Multiple Choice Questions

1. b 160
2. d 160
3. a 160
4. d 161
5. b 161
6. d 161
7. d 161
8. a 162
9. b 162
10. c 162
11. b 162
12. d 163
13. d 163
14. b 163
15. b 163
16. b 163
17. c 163
18. d 164
19. d 164
20. c 164
21. d 164
22. d 165
23. c 165
24. b 165
25. a 165
26. a 165
27. c 166
28. c 166
29. b 166
30. a 166
31. b 167
32. a 167
33. a 168
34. d 169
35. b 169
36. b 169
37. a 169
38. a 170
39. b 170
40. b 171

41. b 171
42. a 171
43. c 171
44. d 172
45. b 172
46. a 173
47. b 173
48. d 173
49. d 173
50. d 173
51. d 173
52. b 175
53. d 175
54. d 176
55. c 176
56. d 176
57. b 178
58. c 179
59. c 180
60. b 180
61. d 181
62. b 181
63. b 183
64. b 186
65. d 186
66. a 186
67. d 186
68. a 187
69. b 186
70. c 186
71. c 187
72. b 187
73. b 187
74. c 188
75. d 190

True-False Questions

1. T 160
2. T 160
3. F 160
4. T 161
5. T 164

6. T 167
7. F 171
8. T 171
9. F 172
10. T 173
11. F 173
12. F 174
13. T 181
14. T 184
15. F 187

Chapter 7
Class and Stratification in the United States

Multiple Choice Questions

1. The "American Dream" is the belief that if people work hard and play by the rules, then they will have a chance to be successful. This idea is based on the assumption of _____.
   a. stratification
   b. inequality
   c. equality
   d. solidarity

2. _____ is the hierarchical arrangement of large social groups based on their control over basic resources and their access to opportunities or life chances.
   a. Income
   b. Prestige
   c. Status
   d. Stratification

3. According to sociologist Max Weber, the term _____ refers to the extent to which individuals have access to important societal resources such as food, clothing, shelter, education, and health care.
   a. meritocracy
   b. alienation
   c. intergenerational mobility
   d. life chances

4. The median household income in the United States is about $40,000. When Congress passed tax cuts in the late 1990's, which of the following annual income groups benefitted most from the cuts?
   a. $0-25,000
   b. $25,001-40,000
   c. $40,001-93,000
   d. greater than $93,000

5. Sociologists distinguish among stratification systems according to whether they are open or closed. Open systems are assumed to have some degree of _____.
   a. slavery
   b. social mobility
   c. socioeconomic status
   d. relative poverty

6. _____ is the movement of individuals or groups from one level in a stratification system to another.
   a. Wealth
   b. Socioeconomic status
   c. Social mobility
   d. Capitalism

7. _____ is the social movement experience by family members from one generation to the next.
   a. Intergenerational mobility
   b. Intragenerational mobility
   c. Economic leveling
   d. Socioeconomic status

8. _____ is the social movement of individuals within their own lifetime.
   a. Intergenerational mobility
   b. Intragenerational mobility
   c. Economic leveling
   d. Socioeconomic status

9. In a closed system of stratification, the boundaries between levels in the hierarchies of social stratification are _____.
   a. easily crossed
   b. rigid
   c. nonexistent
   d. shifting

10. _____ is an extreme form of stratification in which some people are owned by others.
    a. Caste
    b. Class
    c. Slavery
    d. Indemnification

11. During the years of slavery in the United States, slaves were considered to be _____.
    a. property
    b. socially mobile
    c. members of the working class
    d. temporary workers

12. Across the world today, slavery is _____.
    a. permitted in some nations
    b. illegal in all nations
    c. constitutionally permitted in three nations
    d. illegal in only some nations

13. A _____ system is a system of social inequality in which people's status is permanently determined at birth based on their parents' ascribed characteristics.
    a. meritocracy
    b. class
    c. caste
    d. capitalist

14. Slavery, caste, and class are types of _____ systems.
    a. meritocracy
    b. stratification
    c. social mobility
    d. government

15. According to your text, vestiges of caste systems exist today in South Africa and
    _____.
    a. Morocco
    b. Brazil
    c. Greenland
    d. India

16. In a caste system of stratification, social mobility is _____.
    a. easy
    b. inevitable
    c. difficult
    d. almost impossible

17. The _____ system is a type of stratification based on the ownership and control of resources and on the type of work people do.
    a. caste
    b. class
    c. slavery
    d. mobility

18. A _____ system is more open than a caste system because the boundaries between social strata are less distinct.
    a. slavery
    b. mobility
    c. class
    d. structural

19. In a caste system of stratification, one's position in society is almost entirely _____
    a. achieved
    b. ascribed
    c. voluntary
    d. symbolic

20. In _____ systems of stratification, people may become members of a different social stratum than that of their parents.
    a.   slavery
    b.   class
    c.   caste
    d.   closed

21. _____ mobility occurs when people experience a gain or loss in position and/or income that does not produce a change in their place in the class structure.
    a.   Vertical
    b.   Crosscutting
    c.   Horizontal
    d.   Relative

22. Chris' maternal grandparents worked in a cramped sweatshop factory. Her other grandparents quit school to work in a small grocery store. Chris was able to earn a masters degree in Business Administration, and she is now a highly-paid corporate executive. Chris' experience is an example of _____.
    a.   vertical mobility
    b.   crosscutting mobility
    c.   horizontal mobility
    d.   relative mobility

23. Sociologists believe that young people's chances of achieving the American Dream are closely tied to _____.
    a.   how much energy an individual has
    b.   whether or not a person is lazy
    c.   how satisfied their parents were with their jobs
    d.   changing social conditions

24. The social class that Karl Marx called the *bourgeoisie* is made up of _____.
    a.   police officers
    b.   property owners
    c.   propertyless workers
    d.   politicians

25. According to Karl Marx, the *proletariat* is made up of _____.
    a.   foreigners
    b.   property owners
    c.   propertyless workers
    d.   politicians

26. According to Karl Marx, the *bourgeoisie* is _____.
    a. the capitalist class
    b. factory workers
    c. members of labor unions
    d. intellectuals and artists

27. According to Karl Marx, the *proletariat* is _____.
    a. the capitalist class
    b. members of labor unions
    c. the working class
    d. intellectuals and artists

28. Karl Marx believed that the exploitation of workers by the owners initially results in the workers' _____.
    a. formation of labor unions
    b. alienation
    c. respect
    d. search for peaceful political change

29. Karl Marx believed that exploitation of the workers by the owners ultimately results in the workers _____.
    a. giving up the struggle
    b. overthrowing the capitalists
    c. buying the factories they work in
    d. forming political action committees

30. _____ is a feeling of powerlessness and estrangement from other people and from oneself.
    a. Prestige
    b. Alienation
    c. Absolute poverty
    d. Slavery emotion

31. According to Karl Marx, the most important social institution--the one that forms the basis of social class systems of stratification--is _____.
    a. the family
    b. education
    c. government
    d. the economy

32. According to Karl Marx, different social classes have _____ interests.
    a. opposing
    b. complementary
    c. identical
    d. vaguely defined

33.   _____ is the value of all of a person's or family's economic assets including income, personal property, and income-producing property.
    a.   Prestige
    b.   Power
    c.   Wealth
    d.   Economy

34.   _____ is the respect or regard with which a person or status position is regarded by others.
    a.   Prestige
    b.   Power
    c.   Wealth
    d.   Status

35.   _____ is the ability of people or groups to achieve their goals despite opposition from others.
    a.   Prestige
    b.   Power
    c.   Wealth
    d.   Status

36.   _____ refers to a combined measure that attempts to classify individuals, families, or households in terms of factors such as income, occupation, and education to determine class location.
    a.   GNP
    b.   SES
    c.   LVA
    d.   SCI

37.   Max Weber predicted that societies will become more _____ as they gain in size and complexity.
    a.   liberal
    b.   bureaucratic
    c.   unequal
    d.   functional

38.   How many social classes exist in the United States?
    a.   two
    b.   three
    c.   five
    d.   (scholars disagree on this)

39. According to Dennis Gilbert's model of social class, the upper class is also known as the _____ class.
   a. artistic
   b. capitalist
   c. managerial
   d. political

40. Members of the upper class often support the opera, symphony orchestras, the ballet, and art museums, which are examples of _____.
   a. class culture
   b. mass culture
   c. high culture
   d. cultural diffusion

41. Physicians, attorneys, stockbrokers, and corporate managers are highly-educated professionals who are members of the _____ class.
   a. upper-upper
   b. lower-upper
   c. upper-middle
   d. middle

42. Which of the following social classes is the one to which access is most shaped by formal educational attainment?
   a. the upper class
   b. the upper-middle class
   c. the middle class
   d. the working class

43. Today, the entry-level educational requirement for many middle-class occupations such as technicians, nurses, nonretail salesworkers, and legal secretaries is _____.
   a. some high school
   b. a high school diploma
   c. a college degree
   d. a graduate degree

44. Thirty percent of the American population is in the _____ class, which is made up of workers whose job responsibilities involve routine, mechanized tasks requiring little skill beyond basic literacy and a brief period of on-the-job training.
   a. upper
   b. upper-middle
   c. middle
   d. working

45. Sociologists have used the term _____ to refer to relatively low-paying, nonmanual, semiskilled positions primarily held by women, such as day-care workers and cashiers.
   a. second shifters
   b. blue-collar occupations
   c. pink-collar occupations
   d. womens' work

46. The working poor account for about _____ percent of the U.S. population.
   a. 5
   b. 10
   c. 20
   d. 35

47. An estimated _____ percent of the U.S. population is in the working class.
   a. 15
   b. 23
   c. 30
   d. 42

48. Employed single mothers often belong to _____.
   a. the upper middle class
   b. the middle class
   c. the working class
   d. the working poor

49. Social scientists have found that the "missing link" for people on the lowest rung of the social class ladder--the one factor that is essential in order for people to provide for their own needs--is _____.
   a. better on-the-job-training
   b. meaningful employment opportunities
   c. parental training classes
   d. drug treatment programs

50. People in the _____ are poor, seldom employed, and caught in long-term deprivation that results from low levels of education and income and high rates of unemployment.
   a. upper class
   b. middle class
   c. working poor
   d. underclass

51. About 3 to 5 percent of the U.S. population is in the _____.
    a. upper-middle class
    b. midde class
    c. working class
    d. underclass

52. Erik Olin Wright suggests that there are four social classes: the capitalist class, the managerial class, the small-business class, and the _____.
    a. large-business class
    b. executive class
    c. Marxian class
    d. working class

53. According to the *Forbes* Magazine 1999 list of the richest people in the world, _____ was the wealthiest capitalist, with a net worth of $85 billion.
    a. Senator Edward Kennedy
    b. Bill Gates
    c. Martha Stewart
    d. Bob Dole

54. People who have substantial control over the means of production and over workers but who do not participate in key corporate decisions such as how to invest profits, are members of the _____ class.
    a. capitalist
    b. managerial
    c. small-business
    d. working

55. According to Erik Olin Wright's typology of social class, top professionals such as physicians, attorneys, accountants, and engineers are members of the _____ class.
    a. capitalist
    b. managerial
    c. small-business
    d. working

56. Which of the following nations exhibits the greatest amount of inequality of income distribution?
    a. the United States
    b. Canada
    c. New Zealand
    d. Japan

57. According to a recent survey, the net worth of the average white household is _____ times that of the average African American household.
   a. three
   b. five
   c. twelve
   d. twenty-four

58. For most of the richest Americans, _____ is/are a key source of wealth.
   a. wages
   b. end-of-the-year bonuses
   c. inheritance
   d. education

59. More than _____ people in the United States are without health insurance.
   a. 5
   b. 26
   c. 44
   d. 67

60. Persons in which of the following age groups are most likely to be without medical insurance?
   a. 0-6
   b. 7-12
   c. 13-17
   d. 18-24

61. _____ exists when people do not have the means to secure the most basic necessities of life.
   a. Absolute poverty
   b. Relative poverty
   c. Self-fulfilling poverty
   d. Borderline poverty

62. _____ exists when people may be able to afford basic necessities but are still unable to maintain an average standard of living.
   a. Absolute poverty
   b. Relative poverty
   c. Self-fulfilling poverty
   d. Borderline poverty

63. Which of the following groups is most likely to be poor?
   a. white children
   b. African American children
   c. Latino/a children
   d. Persons over age 65

64.   _____ refers to the trend in which women are disproportionately represented among individuals living in poverty.
    a.   Womens' poverty
    b.   Feminization of poverty
    c.   Gender trends
    d.   Sexualization of poverty

65.   On the average, women earn about _____ cents for every dollar that men earn.
    a.   20-30
    b.   40-50
    c.   60-70
    d.   70-80

66.   The risk of poverty for a two-parent African American family is _____ that of a two-parent white family.
    a.   one half
    b.   about the same as
    c.   two times
    d.   six times

67.   Which of the following groups accounts for the largest absolute number of persons who fall below the official poverty line?
    a.   whites
    b.   African Americans
    c.   Latinos/as
    d.   Native Americans

68.   According to the U.S. Bureau of the Census, about _____ percent of African Americans and non-Latinas/os were among the officially poor in 1998, as compared with 10.5 percent of non-Latino/a whites.
    a.   26
    b.   46
    c.   66
    d.   86

69.   Which of the following is a major structural source of poverty, according to the author of your textbook?
    a.   low wages
    b.   a flawed welfare system
    c.   high employment rates
    d.   the national shift from service to manufacturing jobs

70. _____ is a reduction in the proficiency needed to perform a specific job that leads to a corresponding reduction in the wages for that job.
     a.   Job loss
     b.   Job deskilling
     c.   Employment reduction
     d.   Training creep

71. The unemployment rate for African Americans is _____ that of whites.
     a.   half
     b.   about the same as
     c.   double
     d.   six times

72. According to your textbook, about _____ percent of all social welfare benefits are paid to people who do not qualify as poor, such as Social Security recipients who are in the middle and upper income categories.
     a.   20
     b.   40
     c.   60
     d.   80

73. The child poverty rate in the United States is _____ the average of Western European countries.
     a.   half
     b.   about the same as
     c.   four times
     d.   eight times

74. According to Davis and Moore's functionalist approach, social stratification results in _____.
     a.   meritocracy
     b.   exploitation
     c.   no hierarchy of social positions
     d.   rituals

75. According to the _____ perspective, people with economic and political power are able to shape and distribute the rewards, resources, privileges, and opportunities in society for their own benefit.
     a.   functionalist
     b.   conflict
     c.   symbolic interactionist
     d.   (a and c only)

True-False Questions

1. Being poor not only causes economic insecurity, but it also often has negative effects on poor persons' mental and physical health.

2. Women account for two out of three impoverished adults in the United States.

3. Throughout history, five societies have been slave societies. They are ancient Greece, the Roman Empire, the Caribbean, Brazil, and the Congo.

4. In societies whose stratification is based on social class, people are unable to achieve social mobility from one class to another.

5. Karl Marx predicted that workers in capitalist society will rise up and overthrow the government in order to create a more egalitarian society.

6. According to Karl Marx, social class systems of stratification are based primarily on religious ideas.

7. The minimum wage level set by Congress ensures that people who are employed in minimum wage jobs will have sufficient income to cover the cost of housing, food, and the rest of an adult's needs.

8. The old maxim "the rich get richer" is still true in the United States.

9. According to Samuelson and Nordhaus, "If we made an income pyramid out of a child's blocks, with each layer portraying $500 of income, the peak would be far higher than Mount Everest but most people would be within a few feet of the ground."

10. The richest 5 percent of Americans receive approximately 7 percent of all income.

11. In general, people's health status increases as their economic status increases.

12. More-affluent persons tend to be less depressed and face less psychological stress than less affluent persons.

13. One of the most severely economically disadvantaged groups in the United States is Native Americans.

14. According to the author of your text, nearly all persons and groups who receive government benefits are stigmatized and subject to humiliation.

15. Symbolic interactionist William Domhoff has shown how games, rituals, and other activities bind male members of the upper class into a cohesive group.

Chapter 7: Answers to Practice Test Questions

(question-answer-page)

Multiple Choice Questions

1. c 194
2. d 194
3. d 195
4. d 196
5. b 197
6. c 197
7. a 197
8. b 197
9. b 197
10. c 197
11. a 198
12. b 198
13. c 198
14. b 199
15. d 198
16. d 198
17. b 198
18. c 198
19. b 198
20. b 199
21. c 199
22. a 200
23. d 200
24. b 200
25. c 200
26. a 200
27. c 200
28. b 201
29. b 201
30. b 201
31. d 202
32. a 202
33. c 202
34. a 203
35. b 203
36. b 203
37. b 204
38. d 204
39. b 204
40. c 205

41. c 205
42. b 205
43. c 205
44. d 206
45. c 206
46. c 206
47. c 206
48. d 206
49. b 207
50. d 207
51. d 207
52. d 207
53. b 209
54. b 209
55. b 209
56. a 211
57. c 213
58. c 213
59. c 214
60. d 215
61. a 216
62. b 216
63. b 217
64. b 218
65. d 218
66. c 218
67. a 218
68. a 219
69. a 219
70. b 219
71. c 219
72. d 219
73. c 220
74. a 220
75. b 220

True-False Questions

1. T 195
2. T 196
3. F 197
4. F 198
5. T 201

6. F 202
7. F 206
8. T 211
9. T 211
10. F 212
11. T 214
12. T 215
13. T 219
14. F 219
15. T 221

Chapter 8
Global Stratification

Multiple Choice Questions

1. The richest fifth (20 percent) of the world's population receives more than _____ percent of total world income.
    a. 20
    b. 40
    c. 60
    d. 80

2. _____ refers to the unequal distribution of wealth, power, and prestige on a global basis, resulting in people having vastly different lifestyles and life chances both within and among the nations of the world.
    a. Hierarchy
    b. Global stratification
    c. National inequality
    d. Global status

3. Between 1960 and the end of the twentieth century, the gap in global income differences between rich and poor countries _____.
    a. narrowed
    b. remained about the same
    c. widened
    d. was not measurable

4. From which public figure is the following quotation taken? "The poor give us much more than we give them...We don't have to give them pity or sympathy. We have so much to learn from them."
    a. Mother Teresa
    b. President Harry S. Truman
    c. Karl Marx
    d. Mayra Buvini_

5. Most definitions of global inequality are based on _____.
    a. average levels of occupational attainment
    b. levels of income or economic development
    c. levels of educational attainment
    d. measures of population density

6. The United States, Canada, Japan, Great Britain, Australia, and New Zealand are classified by some analysts as _____ nations.
    a.   First World
    b.   Second World
    c.   Third World
    d.   Fourth World

7. Which of the following nations is classified as a Second World country?
    a.   China
    b.   Mozambique
    c.   Ethiopia
    d.   Bangladesh

8. _____ nations are the poorest countries, with little or no industrialization and the lowest standards of living, shortest life expectancies, and highest rates of mortality.
    a.   First World
    b.   Second World
    c.   Third World
    d.   Fourth World

9. _____ nations consist of the rich, industrialized nations that primarily have capitalist economic systems and democratic political systems.
    a.   First World
    b.   Second World
    c.   Third World
    d.   Fourth World

10. Following World War II, the concepts of *underdevelopment* and *underdeveloped nations* emerged out of the _____, which provided massive sums of money in direct aid and loans to rebuild the European economic base destroyed during World War II.
    a.   Lend-Lease plan
    b.   Marshall Plan
    c.   UNICEF program
    d.   CARE program

11. President Harry S. Truman believed that it was necessary to assist the people of economically underdeveloped areas to raise their _____, by which he meant material well-being that can be measured by the quality of goods and services that may be purchased by the per capita national income.
    a.   standard of living
    b.   goods and services index
    c.   Dow Jones Industrial Average
    d.   standard of existence

12. The _____ approach to reducing global poverty assumes that economic growth is the best way to reduce poverty in low-income nations.
    a.   levels of poverty
    b.   culture of poverty
    c.   levels of development
    d.   culture of economics

13. The _____ approach assumes that if nations can increase their Gross National Product (GNP), then social and economic inequality among the citizens within the country can also be reduced.
    a.   levels of poverty
    b.   culture of poverty
    c.   levels of development
    d.   culture of economics

14. Improving a country's GNP often causes inequality within the country to _____.
    a.   decrease greatly
    b.   decrease slightly
    c.   remain about the same
    d.   increase

15. In the low-income, developing nations of the world, the income gap between men and women is _____.
    a.   narrowing rapidly
    b.   narrowing slowly
    c.   remaining about the same
    d.   widening

16. The poorest 40 percent of the Brazilian population receives less than _____ percent of the total national income, whereas the richest 20 percent of the population receives more than 65 percent.
    a.   7
    b.   15
    c.   25
    d.   33

17. Since the U.N. Conference on Environment and Development in Rio de Janeiro in 1992, terms such as *underdevelopment* have largely been dropped in favor of measurements such as sustainable development, and economies are now classified by their levels of

    _____.
    a.   occupational prestige
    b.   education
    c.   income
    d.   infant mortality

18. About _____ of the world's population lives in the fifty-one low-income economies, where most people engage in agricultural pursuits, reside in nonurban areas, and are impoverished.
    a. one-eighth
    b. one-quarter
    c. one-half
    d. three-quarters

19. In 1997 the United States banned imports of goods made by _____.
    a. unmarried women
    b. children in bondage
    c. low-income workers
    d. slaves

20. The Eastern European nations of Armenia and Boznia-Herzegovina may be classified as _____.
    a. low-income
    b. middle-income
    c. high-income
    d. extremely high-income

21. In the high-income, developed nations of the world, the income gap between men and women is _____.
    a. narrowing rapidly
    b. narrowing slowly
    c. remaining about the same
    d. widening

22. About _____ of the world's population resides in the 57 nations with middle-income economies.
    a. one-third
    b. one-half
    c. two-thirds
    d. three-quarters

23. _____ is the movement of jobs and economic resources from one nation to another.
    a. Job transfer
    b. Job loss
    c. Capital flight
    d. Capital transfer

24. _____ is the closing of plants and factories because of their obsolescence or the fact that workers in other nations are being hired to do the work more cheaply.
   a.   Job transfer
   b.   Reindustrialization
   c.   Deindustrialization
   d.   Capital transfer

25. Many middle-income economies have high levels of indebtedness, which reduces the resources available to fight poverty. For example, Uganda spends ___ per person on health care annually, whereas it spends about $17 a person on debt repayment.
   a. $3
   b. $7
   c. $10
   d. $15

26. High-income economies are found in _____ nations of the world.
   a.   5
   b.   15
   c.   25
   d.   50

27. Which of the following nations is among the few lower- and middle-income economies to close the gap with high-income, industrialized economies over the past few decades?
   a.   Ethiopia
   b.   South Korea
   c.   Honduras
   d.   Rwanda

28. The _____ is all the goods and services produced within a country's economy during a given year.
   a.   Gross National Product (GNP)
   b.   Gross Domestic Product (GDP)
   c.   Gross National Income (GNI)
   d.   Gross Domestic Income (GDI)

29. Which of the following is an Asian nation that is heavily populated and home to many poor people?
   a.   Afghanistan
   b.   India
   c.   Madagascar
   d.   New Zealand

30. _____ refers to poverty which exists when people may be able to afford basic necessities but are still unable to maintain an average standard of living (measured by income comparisons).
    a.   Absolute poverty
    b.   Relative poverty
    c.   Subjective poverty
    d.   World poverty

31. According to the World Bank, most of the 700 million "income-poor" people in low- and middle-income nations of the world are _____.
    a.   men
    b.   women
    c.   white
    d.   African-American

32. _____ refers to a condition in which people do not have the means to secure the most basic necessities of life.
    a.   Absolute poverty
    b.   Relative poverty
    c.   Subjective poverty
    d.   World poverty

33. _____ is measured by comparing the actual income against the income earner's expectations and perceptions.
    a.   Absolute poverty
    b.   Relative poverty
    c.   Subjective poverty
    d.   World poverty

34. The measure of income inequality that is used by the World Bank is _____.
    a.   the correlation coefficient
    b.   the Gini coefficient
    c.   the Einstein index
    d.   the Truman index

35. _____ is a measure of income inequality that ranges from zero (meaning that everyone has the same income) to 100 (one person receives all the income).
    a.   the correlation coefficient
    b.   the Gini coefficient
    c.   the Truman index
    d.   the CESD index

36. In 1990 the United Nations Development Program introduced the _____, a new measure of the development level of a country that takes into account life expectancy, education, and living standards.
    a. Gross National Product (GNP)
    b. Gross Domestic Product (GDP)
    c. National Economic Index (NEI)
    d. Human Development Index (HDI)

37. Overall, average life expectancy has _____ in the past three decades.
    a. decreased by one-third
    b. decreased by one-eighth
    c. increased by one-eighth
    d. increased by one-third

38. The average life expectancy at birth of people in middle-income countries is _____ than that of people in high-income countries.
    a. 34 years less
    b. 12 years less
    c. 7 years less
    d. 3 years less

39. The life expectancy of men in Uganda is approximately _____ years.
    a. 36
    b. 43
    c. 51
    d. 65

40. The life expectancy of women in Uganda is approximately _____ years.
    a. 36
    b. 43
    c. 51
    d. 65

41. The average life expectancy of people in low-income nations is as much as _____ than that of people in high-income countries.
    a. 40 years less
    b. 23 years less
    c. 12 years less
    d. 5 years less

42. According to your textbook, one of the major causes of shorter life expectancy in low-income nations is _____.
    a. low educational attainment
    b. high infant mortality
    c. high-fat diets
    d. increased airline travel

43. People in the United States spend about _____ each year on diet products to lower their calorie consumption.
    a. $1 million
    b. $50 million
    c. $5 billion
    d. $100 billion

44. About _____ people die each year from hunger-related diseases.
    a. 10 million
    b. 40 million
    c. 100 million
    d. 3 billion

45. _____ is defined in the Constitution of the World Health Organization as "a state of complete physical, mental and social well-being and not merely the absence of disease or infirmity.
    a. Social justice
    b. World peace
    c. Health
    d. Humanity

46. About _____ people die each year from diarrhea, malaria, tuberculosis, and other infectious and parasitic illnesses.
    a. 3 million
    b. 10 million
    c. 17 million
    d. 37 million

47. Use of tobacco has _____ in low-income and middle-income countries.
    a. greatly decreased
    b. slightly decreased
    c. remained the same
    d. increased

48. A person who can, with understanding, both read and write a short, simple statement on their everyday life meets the United Nations Educational, Scientific, and Cultural Organization (UNESCO) definition of a(n) _____ person.
    a. healthy
    b. literate
    c. middle-income
    d. educated

49. The rate of _____ in the low-income countries is about half that of the high-income countries.
    a. infant mortality
    b. adult deaths
    c. adult literacy
    d. occupational attainment

50. According to the development theory known as _____ theory, global inequality is linked to different levels of economic development, and low-income economies can move to middle- and high-income economies by achieving self-sustained economic growth.
    a. modernization
    b. dependency
    c. world systems
    d. new international division of labor

51. The process of industrialization almost always results in _____ in a nation.
    a. less urbanization
    b. a higher standard of living
    c. a lower standard of living
    d. less social mobility

52. As societies industrialize, they also _____ as workers locate their residencies near factories, offices, and other places of work.
    a. become larger
    b. become more urbanized
    c. become more family-oriented
    d. become more suburban

53. According to modernization theory, the values and attitudes of people in developing countries become _____ those of people in high-income nations.
    a. vastly different from
    b. slightly different from
    c. more similar to
    d. identical to

54. According to Walt Rostow's version of modernization theory, all countries go through four stages of economic development. In the _____ stage, a period of economic growth occurs, along with a growing belief in individualism, competition, and achievement.
    a. traditional
    b. take-off
    c. technological maturity
    d. high mass consumption

55. According to Walt Rostow's version of modernization theory, all countries go through four stages of economic development. In the _____ stage, the highest standard of living is reached.
    a. traditional
    b. take-off
    c. technological maturity
    d. high mass consumption

56. According to Walt Rostow's version of modernization theory, all countries go through four stages of economic development. In the _____ stage, very little social change takes place because people hold to a fatalistic value system, do not subscribe to the work ethic, and save very little money.
    a. traditional
    b. take-off
    c. technological maturity
    d. high mass consumption

57. Modernization theory has been criticized for being _____.
    a. communist
    b. eurocentric
    c. socialist
    d. anti-capitalist

58. _____ theory states that global poverty can at least partially be attributed to the fact that the low-income countries have been exploited by the high-income countries.
    a. World systems
    b. Dependency
    c. Modernization
    d. The new international division of labor

59. Which of the following theoretical approaches to global inequality most closely approximates a functionalist explanation?
    a. new international division of labor theory
    b. world systems theory
    c. dependency theory
    d. modernization theory

60. _____ theory assumes that how a country is incorporated into the global capitalist economy (e.g., a core, semiperipheral, or peripheral nation) is the key feature in determining how economic development takes place in that nation.
    a. World systems
    b. Dependency
    c. Modernization
    d. The new international division of labor

61. _____ theory assumes that commodity production is split into fragments, each of which can be moved (e.g., by a transnational corporation) to whichever part of the world can provide the best combination of capital and labor.
    a. World systems
    b. Dependency
    c. Modernization
    d. The new international division of labor

62. According to world systems theory, _____ nations are dependent on core nations for capital, have little or no industrialization (other than what may be brought in by core nations), and have uneven patterns of urbanization.
    a. peripheral
    b. semiperiheral
    c. central
    d. border

63. According to world systems theory, _____ nations are dominant capitalist centers characterized by high levels of industrialization and urbanization.
    a. core
    b. peripheral
    c. semiperipheral
    d. Third World

64. World systems theory is based on _____ ideas about global imperialism and economic exploitation.
    a. Emile Durkheim's
    b. Mother Teresa's
    c. Karl Marx's
    d. Bill Gates'

65. Which of the following is a core nation, according to world systems theory?
    a. South Korea
    b. Brazil
    c. Nigeria
    d. Germany

66. Which of the following is a semiperipheral nation, according to world systems theory?
    a. United States
    b. Japan
    c. Germany
    d. Taiwan

67. Most low-income countries in Africa, South America, and the Caribbean may be classified as _____ nations, according to world systems theory.
    a. core
    b. peripheral
    c. semiperipheral
    d. border

68. Superior Product Company is a transnational corporation that has closed its manufacturing plants in Arizona and opened plants in Mexico because labor costs and taxes are cheaper there and environmental regulations are less strict. This most closely illustrates the assumptions of _____.
    a. world systems
    b. dependency
    c. modernization
    d. new international division of labor

69. Transnational corporations have built _____ plants (factories) so that goods can be assembled in Mexico by low-wage workers to keep production costs down, after which the goods are sent back to the United States for sale.
    a. *maquiladora*
    b. *hacienda*
    c. *San Diego*
    d. *Tex-Mex*

70. _____ refers to a complex pattern of international labor and production processes that results in a finished commodity ready for sale in the marketplace.
    a. Global inequality links
    b. Global commodity chains
    c. International labor agreements
    d. Organized labor decrees

71. _____ is the term used to describe industries in which transnational corporations play a central part in controlling the production process.
    a. Producer-driven commodity chains
    b. Buyer-driven commodity chains
    c. Core national industries
    d. Peripheral national industries

72. _____ is the term used to refer to industries in which large retailers, brand name merchandizers, and trading companies set up decentralized production networks in various middle- and low-income countries.
    a. Producer-driven commodity chains
    b. Buyer-driven commodity chains
    c. Core national industries
    d. Peripheral national industries

73. According to the new international division of labor theory, athletic footwear companies such as Nike and Reebok and clothing companies like The Gap and Liz Claiborne are examples of the _____ model.
   a. producer-driven commodity chains
   b. buyer-driven commodity chains
   c. core national industries
   d. peripheral national industries

74. Workers in _____ are often exploited by low wages, long hours, and poor working conditions. Most workers cannot afford to buy the product that they make.
   a. buyer-driven commodity chains
   b. producer-driven commodity chains
   c. core nations
   d. high-income nations

75. Tina Alwin works on an assembly line at a Reebok tennis shoe factory in Indonesia. Since she earns the equivalent of $1.28 per day, her monthly income would fall short of the price of one pair of the shoes that she makes. Her situation illustrates some of the problems in _____.
   a. buyer-driven commodity chains
   b. producer-driven commodity chains
   c. transnational corporations
   d. unionized factories

True-False Questions

1. The richest fifth of the world's population receives about 50 percent of the total world income.

2. The majority of people with incomes below the poverty line live in rural areas of the world.

3. Between 1960 and the end of the twentieth century, the gap in global income differences between rich and poor countries widened.

4. The primary business of the World Bank is to provide loans and policy advice to low- and middle-income member countries.

5. *Absolute poverty* is defined as the number of people who are unable to afford basic necessities but are still able to maintain an average standard of living.

6. The average income per person in the world's low-income countries has doubled over the past 25 years.

7.   Through the efforts of the United Nations and other human services organizations, effective treatments for all known infectious diseases have been developed.

8.   Most of the poor people of the world are women and children.

9.   Modernization theory implicity tends to view low-income countries as backward.

10.   World Systems Theory is based primarily on the ideas of Emile Durkheim.

11.   World Systems Theory classifies nations into three types: core nations, rich nations, and moderate nations.

12.   Immanuel Wallerstein, developer of World Systems Theory, acknowledges that the theory is an incomplete explanation.

13.   The richest person in the world is a citizen of China.

14.   One of the most pressing problems in peripheral nations is a shortage of housing.

15.   Nearly all social scientists agree that global inequality will decrease sharply in the next few decades.

Chapter 8: Answers to Practice Test Questions

(question-answer-page)

Multiple Choice Questions

1. d 228	41. b 238	6. T 238
2. b 227	42. b 238	7. F 240
3. c 229	43. c 239	8. T 240
4. a 229	44. b 239	9. T 242
5. b 230	45. c 239	10. F 244
6. a 230	46. c 239	11. F 244
7. a 230	47. d 240	12. T 246
8. c 230	48. b 240	13. F 245
9. a 230	49. c 240	14. T 246
10. b 231	50. a 241	15. F 248
11. a 231	51. b 241	
12. c 231	52. b 241	
13. c 231	53. c 241	
14. d 231	54. b 241	
15. d 233	55. d 242	
16. a 231	56. a 241	
17. c 232	57. b 242	
18. c 232	58. b 242	
19. b 233	59. d 242	
20. a 233	60. a 243	
21. d 233	61. d 243	
22. a 233	62. a 245	
23. c 234	63. a 244	
24. c 234	64. c 244	
25. a 234	65. d 244	
26. c 234	66. d 245	
27. b 235	67. b 245	
28. b 236	68. d 246	
29. b 237	69. c 245	
30. b 237	70. b 247	
31. b 238	71. a 247	
32. a 237	72. b 247	
33. c 237	73. b 247	
34. b 237	74. a 247	
35. b 237	75. a 247	
36. d 238		
37. d 238	**True-False Questions**	
38. b 238	1. F 228	
39. b 238	2. T 228	
40. b 238	3. T 229	
	4. T 232	
	5. F 237	

Chapter 9
Race and Ethnicity

Multiple Choice Questions

1. A(n) _____ is a category of people who have been singled out as inferior or superior, often on the basis of real or alleged physical characteristics such as skin color, hair texture, eye shape, or other subjectively selected attributes.
    a.   ethnic group
    b.   status group
    c.   cohort
    d.   race

2. Social scientists view race as _____.
    a.   a biological fact
    b.   a socially constructed category
    c.   an ethnic category
    d.   an objective classification

3. How many human racial groups are there, according to social scientists?
    a.   two
    b.   three
    c.   five
    d.   (racial classifications are not biologically valid)

4. A(n) _____ is a collection of people distinguished, by others or by themselves, primarily on the basis of cultural or nationality characteristics.
    a.   ethnic group
    b.   status group
    c.   cohort
    d.   race

5. To classify people as Italian American, Jewish American, or Irish American is to classify them according to their _____.
    a.   ethnic group
    b.   status group
    c.   cohort
    d.   race

6. Which of the following characteristics is/are shared by members of a certain ethnic group?
    a.   a feeling of ethnocentrism
    b.   a sense of community
    c.   ascribed membership from birth
    d.   (all of the above are shared by members of a particular ethnic group)

7. To social scientists, race and ethnicity are important because they _____.
   a. reflect important genetic differences between people
   b. are related to innate intelligence
   c. influence how people act toward other people
   d. determine people's biological limitations

8. A _____ is one that is advantaged and has superior resources and rights in a society.
   a. minority group
   b. majority group
   c. racial group
   d. ethnic group

9. A _____ is one whose members, because of physical or cultural characteristics, are disadvantaged, are subject to unequal treatment by the dominant group, and regard themselves as objects of collective discrimination.
   a. minority group
   b. majority group
   c. racial group
   d. ethnic group

10. Which of the following groups is considered to be the *majority group* in North America?
    a. WASPs
    b. DINKs
    c. Yuppies
    d. women

11. Which of the following is considered to be a *minority group* in North America?
    a. Yuppies
    b. white women
    c. DINKs
    d. white men

12. The terms *majority group* and *minority group* imply that one group _____ the other group.
    a. contains more members who are adults than
    b. has more power than
    c. is biologically inferior to
    d. is equal to

13. _____ is a negative attitude based on faulty generalizations about members of selected racial and ethnic groups.
    a. Discrimination
    b. Prejudice
    c. Stigma
    d. Judgement

14. Prejudice _____.
    a. is always negative
    b. is always positive
    c. can be positive or negative
    d. is neither positive nor negative

15. A(n) _____ is an overgeneralization about the appearance, behavior or other characteristics of members of particular categories.
    a. ethnocentrism
    b. stereotype
    c. stigma
    d. discrimination

16. The use of Native American names for sports teams, such as the Atlanta Braves, Cleveland Indians, Washington Redskins, and City High School Warriors, is based on _____.
    a. bilingualism
    b. stereotypes
    c. discrimination
    d. assimilation

17. Sports fans' use of Native American chants, war painted costumes, and gestures like the Atlanta Braves' "tomahawk chop," is based on _____.
    a. bilingualism
    b. stereotypes
    c. discrimination
    d. assimilation

18. _____ is a set of attitudes, beliefs, and practices that is used to justify the superior treatment of one racial or ethnic group and the inferior treatment of another racial or ethnic group.
    a. Prejudice
    b. Discrimination
    c. Racism
    d. Sexism

19. The late Al Campanis, former Los Angeles Dodgers General Manager, repeatedly stated on national television that African Americans "lacked the necessities" to handle coaching and management positions. This is an example of _____.
    a. subtle racism
    b. overt racism
    c. subtle discrimination
    d. overt discrimination

20. In a conversation at home, the coach of a football team tells his wife that African American players have "natural" abilities in terms of speed and agility, but that they do not have the ability to perform leadership roles. This is an example of _____.
    a. subtle racism
    b. overt racism
    c. subtle discrimination
    d. overt discrimination

21. Members of subordinate racial and ethnic groups are often blamed for societal problems, such as unemployment or economic recession, over which they have no control. This is an example of _____.
    a. the authoritarian personality
    b. institutional discrimination
    c. small-group discrimination
    d. scapegoating

22. According to symbolic interactionists, prejudice results from _____.
    a. genetic inheritance
    b. social learning
    c. objective differences between groups
    d. discrimination

23. _____ is characterized by excessive conformity, submissiveness to authority, intolerance, insecurity, a high level of superstition, and rigid, stereotyped thinking.
    a. Prejudice
    b. Discrimination
    c. The Ethnocentric Personality
    d. The Authoritarian Personality

24. _____ involves actions or practices of dominant group members (or their representatives) that have a harmful impact on members of a subordinate group.
    a. Prejudice
    b. Discrimination
    c. Assimilation
    d. Ethnic pluralism

25. According to sociologist Robert Merton's classification, _____ are not personally prejudiced and do not discriminate against others.
    a. Unprejudiced nondiscriminators
    b. Unprejudiced discriminators
    c. Prejudiced nondiscriminators
    d. Prejudiced discriminators

26. According to sociologist Robert Merton's classification, _____ hold personal prejudices and actively discriminate against others.
    a. Unprejudiced nondiscriminators
    b. Unprejudiced discriminators
    c. Prejudiced nondiscriminators
    d. Prejudiced discriminators

27. According to sociologist Robert Merton's classification, _____ hold personal prejudices but do not discriminate due to peer pressure, legal demands, or a desire for profits.
    a. Unprejudiced nondiscriminators
    b. Unprejudiced discriminators
    c. Prejudiced nondiscriminators
    d. Prejudiced discriminators

28. According to sociologist Robert Merton's classification, _____ may have no personal prejudice but still engage in discriminatory behavior because of peer group pressure or economic, political, or social interests.
    a. Unprejudiced nondiscriminators
    b. Unprejudiced discriminators
    c. Prejudiced nondiscriminators
    d. Prejudiced discriminators

29. Prejudice is a(n) _____.
    a. action
    b. attitude
    c. behavior
    d. artifact

30. The ultimate form of discrimination is _____.
    a. genocide
    b. fratricide
    c. homicide
    d. assault

31. The new term "ethnic cleansing" describes a form of _____.
    a. genocide
    b. prejudice
    c. assimilation
    d. superstition

32. _____ consists of one-on-one acts by members of the dominant group that harm members of the subordinate group or their property.
    a. Individual prejudice
    b. Institutional prejudice
    c. Individual discrimination
    d. Institutional discrimination

33. If a landlord decides not to rent an apartment to a couple after he learns that they are African American, this is an example of _____.
    a. individual prejudice
    b. institutional prejudice
    c. individual discrimination
    d. institutional discrimination

34. _____ consists of the day-to-day practices of organizations and institutions that have a harmful impact on members of subordinate groups.
    a. Individual prejudice
    b. Institutional prejudice
    c. Individual discrimination
    d. Institutional discrimination

35. First National Bank consistently denies loans to persons who are Native American. This is an example of _____.
    a. individual prejudice
    b. institutional prejudice
    c. individual discrimination
    d. institutional discrimination

36. A prejudiced judge gives harsher sentences to all African American defendants but he is not supported by the judicial system in these actions. According to sociologist Joe R. Feagin's classification, this is an example of _____.
    a. isolate discrimination
    b. small-group discrimination
    c. direct institutionalized discrimination
    d. indirect institutionalized discrimination

37. Special education classes are intended to provide extra educational opportunities to children with various types of disabilities. However, special education classes may have contributed to racial stereotyping that tells young people of color that "they will not make it in life, so why even try." According to sociologist Joe R. Feagin's classification, this is an example of _____.
    a. isolate discrimination
    b. small-group discrimination
    c. direct institutionalized discrimination
    d. indirect institutionalized discrimination

38. In the American South during the Jim Crow era, African Americans were excluded by law from eating in white-only restaurants, riding in the front of public buses, and using white-only waiting rooms. According to sociologist Joe R. Feagin's classification, this is an example of _____.
    a. isolate discrimination
    b. small-group discrimination
    c. direct institutionalized discrimination
    d. indirect institutionalized discrimination

39. A group of five white students deface a professor's office door with racist epithets, but the students do not have the support of other students or faculty members. According to sociologist Joe R. Feagin's classification, this is an example of _____.
    a. isolate discrimination
    b. small-group discrimination
    c. direct institutionalized discrimination
    d. indirect institutionalized discrimination

40. In the _____ hypothesis, symbolic interactionists point out that contact between people from divergent groups should lead to favorable attitudes and behavior when certain factors are present. Members of each group must 1) have equal status, (2) pursue the same goals, (3) cooperate with one another to achieve their goals, and (4) receive positive feedback when they interact with one another in positive, nondiscriminatory ways.
    a. feedback
    b. interaction
    c. goals
    d. contact

41. When individuals meet someone who does not conform to the stereotype they have of that "type" of person, they often view the person as a(n) _____.
    a. example
    b. exception
    c. assimilation
    d. criminal

42. _____ is a process by which members of subordinate racial and ethnic groups become absorbed into the dominant culture.
    a. Colonialism
    b. Pluralism
    c. Migration
    d. Assimilation

43. _____ assimilation, or acculturation, occurs when members of an ethnic group adopt dominant group traits, such as language, dress, values, religion, and food preferences.
    a. Psychological
    b. Biological
    c. Structural
    d. Cultural

44. _____ assimilation, or amalgamation, occurs when members of one group marry those of other social or ethnic groups.
    a. Psychological
    b. Biological
    c. Structural
    d. Cultural

45. _____ assimilation, or integration, occurs when members of subordinate racial or ethnic groups gain acceptance in everyday social interaction with members of the dominant group.
    a. Psychological
    b. Biological
    c. Structural
    d. Cultural

46. _____ assimilation involves a change in racial or ethnic self-identification on the part of an individual.
    a. Psychological
    b. Biological
    c. Structural
    d. Cultural

47. _____ is the coexistence of a variety of distinct racial and ethnic groups within one society.
    a. Assimilation
    b. Colonialism
    c. Ethnic Pluralism
    d. Ethnic Migration

48. _____ is the spatial and social separation of categories of people by race, ethnicity, class, gender, and/or religion.
    a. Genocide
    b. Colonialism
    c. Migration
    d. Segregation

49. _____ segregation is segregation that is enforced by law.
    a. *De facto*
    b. *De jure*
    c. Legalistic
    d. Juridical

50. Racial separation and inequality enforced by custom rather than law is known as _____ segregation.
    a. *de facto*
    b. *de jure*
    c. legalistic
    d. juridical

51. Enforced segregation by race in housing sales has been declared unconstitutional by the U.S. Supreme Court. However, residential segregation is still common in many parts of the country as owners, landlords, real estate agents, and apartment managers maintain their properties for whites only. This is an example of _____ segregation.
    a. *de facto*
    b. *de jure*
    c. legalistic
    d. juridical

52. One variation of the conflict theory approach views racial and ethnic inequality as a permanent feature of U.S. society. Since African Americans were the only people who were enslaved, a _____ system was instituted even after slavery was abolished by law.
    a. caste
    b. class
    c. prestige
    d. status

53. Miscegenation laws prohibit sexual intercourse or marriage between persons of different _____.
    a. ages
    b. religions
    c. races
    d. geographic origins

54. _____ occurs when members of a racial or ethnic group are conquered or colonized and forcibly placed under the economic and political control of the dominant group.
    a. Class warfare
    b. Caste warfare
    c. Internal colonialism
    d. External colonialism

55. According to the _____ theoretical perspective, sports reflect the interests of the wealthy and powerful classes.
    a. functionalist
    b. conflict
    c. symbolic interactionist
    d. split-labor-market

56. According to the _____ theoretical perspective, the economy is divided into two areas of employment--a primary sector or upper tier, composed of higher-paid (usually dominant group) workers in more secure jobs, and a secondary sector or lower tier, composed of lower-paid (often subordinate group) workers in jobs with little security and hazardous working conditions.
    a. functionalist
    b. symbolic interactionist
    c. split-labor-market
    d. pluralist

57. The term _____ refers to the interactive effect of racism and sexism in the exploitation of women of color.
    a. assimilation
    b. gendered sexism
    c. gendered racism
    d. ageist racism

58. The Naturalization law of 1790 permitted only _____ immigrants to apply for naturalization (become U.S. citizens).
    a. African-Americans
    b. white
    c. Asians
    d. Catholics

59. _____ states that actions of the government substantially define racial and ethnic relations in the United States. These actions range from passage of race-related legislation to the imprisonment of members of groups believed to be a threat to society.
    a. The theory of racial formation
    b. The theory of social class
    c. Race relations theory
    d. Inequality theory

60. According to _____, racism is such an ingrained feature of U.S. society that it appears to be ordinary and natural to many people.
    a. functionalist theory
    b. symbolic interactionist theory
    c. critical race theory
    d. ethnic critique theory

61. According to the legal scholar Derrick Bell, white elites tolerate or encourage racial advances for people of color *only* if the dominant group members believe that their own self-interest will be served in so doing. This assumption is known as _____.
    a. racial formation
    b. the inequality hypothesis
    c. status interest
    d. interest convergence

62. Critical race theory is similar to _____ approaches in that it calls our attention to the fact that things are not always as they seem.
    a. functionalist
    b. postmodernist
    c. assimilationist
    d. ethnic pluralism

63. It is estimated that approximately _____ Native Americans were living in North America at the time of Columbus' voyage in 1492, although their numbers were reduced to less than 240,000 by 1900.
    a. 500,000
    b. 2 million
    c. 4 million
    d. 10 million

64. Europeans and other white settlers (or invaders) often justified their aggression against Native Americans by casting them as "savages" and "heathens." This is an example of _____.
    a. forced migration
    b. forced assimilation
    c. segregation
    d. stereotyping

65. In the winter of 1832, over half of the Cherokee Nation died during or as a result of their forced relocation from the southeastern United States to the Indian Territory in Oklahoma. This instance of forced relocation is known as the _____.
    a. "Dying Time"
    b. "Trail of Tears"
    c. "Native American Holocaust"
    d. "Sadness Trail"

66. After the American Revolution, the government of the United States broke treaty after treaty as it engaged in a policy of wholesale removal of indigenous Native American nations in order to _____.
    a. protect the land from environmental damage
    b. provide Native Americans with a better life
    c. clear the land for settlement by whites
    d. protect Native Americans from danger

67. By 1920, about _____ percent of former Native American lands had been taken over by the U.S. government or by state governments.
    a. 20
    b. 48
    c. 60
    d. 98

68. After 1871, many Native American children were required to attend schools operated by the United States Bureau of Indian Affairs in order to hasten their transition into members of the dominant culture. The government's attempt to socialize Native American children into the norms and values of the dominant culture was an attempt to achieve

    _____.
    a. assimilation
    b. pluralism
    c. genocide
    d. colonialism

69. The life expectancy of Native American men who live on reservations is approximately _____ years.
    a. 35
    b. 45
    c. 55
    d. 65

70. Descendants of British immigrants to the U.S. are sometimes referred to as WASPs. This acronym stands for _____.
    a. Wealthy Anglo Saxon Participant
    b. Wealthy And Socially Prominent
    c. White And Specially Privileged
    d. White Anglo Saxon Protestant

71. According to Table 9.1 in your textbook, which of the following racial or ethnic groups is not represented in any professional sport except football?
    a. African Americans
    b. Latino/as
    c. Native Americans
    d. Asian Americans

72. The rate of unemployment for African Americans is approximately _____ that of whites.
    a. half
    b. equal to
    c. twice
    d. six times

73. The term _____ is applied to a wide diversity of immigrants who trace their origins to Ireland and to eastern and southern European countries such as Poland, Italy, Greece, Germany, Yugoslavia, and Russia and the other former Soviet republics.
   a. WASPs
   b. white ethnic Americans
   c. second-generation immigrants
   d. WEEA's

74. The Census Bureau uses the term _____ to designate the many diverse groups with roots in Asia and the Pacific Islands.
   a. Indochinese
   b. Asian Americans
   c. Orientals
   d. Koreans

75. Since 1970, many immigrants have arrived in the United States from countries located in _____, which is the geographic region from Afghanistan to Libya and includes Arabia, Cyprus and Asiatic Turkey.
   a. Southeast Asia
   b. the Middle East
   c. Eastern Europe
   d. the Caucasus

True-False Questions

1. Social scientists agree that there are three biological races of humans.

2. Discrimination is an attitude, while prejudice is a behavior.

3. According to the class perspective of sociologist Oliver C. Cox, African Americans were enslaved because they were the cheapest and best workers the owners could find for heavy labor in the mines and on plantations. Thus the profit motive of capitalists, not skin color or racial prejudice, accounted for slavery.

4. According to conflict theorists, sports (at all levels) exploits athletes (even highly paid ones) in order to gain high levels of profit and prestige for coaches, managers, and owners.

5. Native Americans have been the victims of genocide at the hands of the United States.

6. WASP women enjoy the privileges of a dominant racial position, along with equality of gender-related rights with WASP men.

7. The 1996 case of *Hopwood v. State of Texas*, heard in the U.S. Fifth Circuit Court of Appeals, held that college and university Affirmative Action programs that use race as a factor in admissions decisions are illegal.

8. The term that is commonly used to refer to prejudice, hostile attitudes, and discriminatory behavior against Jewish persons is *anti-Jewish behavior.*

9. The Chinese Exclusion Act of 1882 brought immigration from China to a halt until the Act was repealed during World War II.

10. Today, Filipino Americans constitute the second largest category of Asian Americans, with over a million population in the United States.

11. Terms *Latino* (for males) and *Latina* (for females) and *Hispanic* are used interchangeably to refer to people who trace their origins to Spanish-speaking Latin America and the Iberian peninsula.

12. The largest segment of the Latino/a population in the United States is made up of people with Puerto Rican ancestry.

13. Since 1917, all persons born in Puerto Rico hold U.S. citizenship.

14. Throughout the world, most racial and ethnic groups have chosen to reject the goal of *self-determination.*

15. Scholars predict that, by the middle of the 21st century, white Americans will constitute approximately 85 percent of U.S. residents.

Chapter 9: Answers to Practice Test Questions

(question-answer-page)

Multiple Choice Questions

1. d 254	41. b 260	6. F 268
2. b 254	42. d 261	7. T 271
3. d 254	43. d 261	8. F 273
4. a 254	44. b 261	9. T 274
5. a 254	45. c 261	10. T 275
6. d 254	46. a 261	11. T 277
7. c 255	47. c 262	12. F 277
8. b 255	48. d 262	13. T 277
9. a 255	49. b 262	14. F 279
10. a 255	50. a 262	15. F 279
11. b 255	51. a 262	
12. b 255	52. a 262	
13. b 255	53. c 262	
14. c 256	54. c 263	
15. b 257	55. b 263	
16. b 257	56. c 264	
17. b 257	57. c 264	
18. c 257	58. b 264	
19. b 257	59. a 265	
20. a 257	60. c 265	
21. d 258	61. d 265	
22. b 258	62. b 265	
23. d 258	63. b 265	
24. b 258	64. d 265	
25. a 258	65. b 265	
26. d 258	66. c 265	
27. c 258	67. d 266	
28. b 258	68. a 266	
29. b 258	69. b 267	
30. a 259	70. d 268	
31. a 259	71. c 269	
32. c 259	72. c 272	
33. c 259	73. b 273	
34. d 259	74. b 274	
35. d 259	75. b 278	
36. a 259		
37. d 259	**True-False Questions**	
38. c 259	1. F 253	
39. b 259	2. F 258	
40. d 260	3. T 262	
	4. T 263	
	5. T 265	

132

Chapter 10
Sex and Gender

Multiple Choice Questions

1. The prevalence among American women of eating disorders is due in large part to
    _____.
    a. biological factors
    b. psychological factors
    c. environmental factors
    d. cultural factors

2. _____ is the process of treating people as if they were objects or things, not human beings.
    a. Gentrification
    b. Demonization
    c. Demoralization
    d. Objectification

3. Women in the United States and other nations are particularly likely to be the targets of
    _____.
    a. gentrification
    b. demonization
    c. demoralization
    d. objectification

4. Sociologist Sharlene Hesse-Bieber points to the existence of a(n) _____, in which people (usually women) worship the "perfect" body and engage in rituals such as dieting and exercising with "obsessive attention to monitoring progress..."
    a. interaction ritual
    b. cult of thinness
    c. body cult
    d. food and exercise obsession

5. Body image results in large part from _____.
    a. cultural definitions of attractiveness
    b. psychological differences between men and women
    c. biological differences among men and women
    d. inherited factors

6. Joe often refers to attractive women as "a piece of ass." This is an example of
    _____.
    a. gentrification
    b. demonization
    c. demoralization
    d. objectification

7.   _____ refers to the distinctive qualities of men and women (masculinity and femininity) that are culturally created.
   a.   Gender
   b.   Sex
   c.   Biology
   d.   Destiny

8.   _____ refers to the biological and anatomical differences between females and males.
   a.   Gender
   b.   Sex
   c.   Evolution
   d.   Differentiation

9.   Which of the following is an example of *primary sex characteristics*?
   a.   pubic hair
   b.   enlarged breasts
   c.   wider hips
   d.   genitalia

10.   Which of the following combination of chromosomes will result in a normal male embryo?
   a.   XX
   b.   XY
   c.   XXY
   d.   XYY

11.   Which of the following combination of chromosomes will result in a normal female embryo?
   a.   XX
   b.   XY
   c.   XXY
   d.   XYY

12.   A _____ is a person in whom sexual differentiation is ambiguous or incomplete, and who tends to have some combination of male and female genitalia.
   a.   transsexual
   b.   transvestite
   c.   lesbian
   d.   hermaphrodite

13. A _____ is a person in whom the sex-related structures of the brain that define gender identity are opposite from the physical sex organs of the person's body.
   a. transsexual
   b. transvestite
   c. lesbian
   d. hermaphrodite

14. A _____ is a male who lives as a woman or a female who lives as a man but does not alter the genitalia.
   a. transsexual
   b. transvestite
   c. lesbian
   d. hermaphrodite

15. Some societies recognize a sexual category known as *berdaches*, *hijras* or *xaniths*. Which of the following terms would best describe a person in one of these categories?
   a. transsexual
   b. transvestite
   c. lesbian
   d. hermaphrodite

16. _____ refers to an individual's preference for emotional-sexual relationships with members of the opposite sex, the same sex, or both.
   a. Heterosexuality
   b. Homosexuality
   c. Sexual orientation
   d. Sexual involvement

17. In the 1990s, the term _____ was created to describe individuals whose appearance, behavior, or self-identification does not conform to common social rules of gender expression.
   a. lesbian
   b. homosexual
   c. transgender
   d. transvestite

18. According to research carried out at the University of Chicago, persons who have engaged in one act of homosexuality are _____.
   a. gay
   b. straight
   c. bisexual
   d. (one act does not determine a person's sexual identity)

19. Extreme prejudice directed at gays, lesbians, bisexuals, and others who are perceived as not being heterosexual is known as _____.
    a. discrimination
    b. hate crime
    c. homophobia
    d. sexual phobia

20. Recent studies show that up to _____ percent of men express dissatisfaction with some aspect of their bodies.
    a. 35
    b. 55
    c. 75
    d. 95

21. _____ refers to the attitudes, behaviors, and activities that are socially defined as appropriate for each sex and are learned through the socialization process.
    a. Sexual identity
    b. Gender role
    c. Gender identity
    d. Body consciousness

22. According to sociologists, the most important determinant of what males and females are expected to do is/are _____.
    a. social and cultural processes
    b. biological factors
    c. matriarchy
    d. sexual orientation

23. In U.S. society, men are traditionally expected to demonstrate aggressiveness and toughness, whereas females are expected to be passive and nurturing. This is an example of _____.
    a. sexual identity
    b. gender role
    c. gender identity
    d. body consciousness

24. _____ is a person's perception of the self as female or male.
    a. Gender role
    b. Sexual characteristics
    c. Gender identity
    d. Sexual functioning

25. Every society uses gender to assign certain tasks to males and females, and differentially rewards those who perform these tasks. Sociologists refer to structural features, external to the individual, that perpetuate gender inequality as _____.
   a. social institutions
   b. sex roles
   c. primary sex characteristics
   d. gendered institutions

26. Gender _____ hold(s) that men and women are inherently different in attributes, behavior, and aspirations.
   a. stratification
   b. perspectives
   c. consciousness
   d. stereotypes

27. The eating disorder known as _____ is defined as loss of at least 25 percent of body weight due to a compulsive fear of becoming fat.
   a. obesity
   b. anorexia
   c. bulimia
   d. food phobia

28. The eating disorder known as _____ occurs when a person binges by consuming large quantities of food and then purges the food by induced vomiting, excessive exercise, laxatives, or fasting.
   a. obesity
   b. anorexia
   c. bulimia
   d. food phobia

29. The most common victims of eating disorders tend to be _____.
   a. children
   b. women
   c. men
   d. the elderly

30. _____ is the subordination of one sex, usually female, based on the assumed superiority of the other sex.
   a. Sexism
   b. Matriarchy
   c. Stratification
   d. Inequality

31.   Like racism, sexism is used to justify harmful acts known as _____.
        a.   prejudice
        b.   discrimination
        c.   stratification
        d.   body consciousness

32.   _____ is a hierarchical system of social organization in which cultural, political, and economic structures are controlled by men.
        a.   Gender organization
        b.   Pastoralism
        c.   Patriarchy
        d.   Matriarchy

33.   _____ is a hierarchical system of social organization in which cultural, political, and economic structures are controlled by women.
        a.   Gender organization
        b.   Pastoralism
        c.   Patriarchy
        d.   Matriarchy

34.   A society where men are seen as "natural" heads of households, presidential candidates, corporate executives, college presidents, etc., and where women are men's subordinates is an example of a _____.
        a.   Sexual society
        b.   Pastoral society
        c.   Patriarchy
        d.   Matriarchy

35.   Which of the following is found in nearly every society across the world?
        a.   matriarchy
        b.   horticulturalism
        c.   pastoralism
        d.   patriarchy

36.   In which of the following types of society do people grow their own food, and use hand tools such as the digging stick and the hoe?
        a.   hunting and gathering societies
        b.   horticultural and pastoral societies
        c.   agrarian societies
        d.   industrial societies

37. In which of the following types of society do women enjoy relatively equal status with men?
    a.   hunting and gathering societies
    b.   horticultural and pastoral societies
    c.   agrarian societies
    d.   industrial societies

38. In industrial and postindustrial societies, inheritance of property tends to be _____ .
    a.   neolocal
    b.   patrilocal
    c.   matrilineal
    d.   patrilineal

39. A _____ society is one in which technology supports a service- and information-based economy.
    a.   horticultural and pastoral
    b.   agrarian
    c.   industrial
    d.   postindustrial

40. Formal education is increasingly crucial for economic and social success of both women and men in _____ societies.
    a.   horticultural and pastoral
    b.   agrarian
    c.   industrial
    d.   postindustrial

41. Studies indicate that children's toys reflect their parents' _____ .
    a.   age in the life course
    b.   sex differentiation
    c.   gender expectations
    d.   religious affiliation

42. From birth, parents act toward children on the basis of the child's sex. In this way they influence the role development of children by passing on their own beliefs about gender. This process is known as _____ .
    a.   life course education
    b.   gender socialization
    c.   sex socialization
    d.   gender education

43. Research by sociologist Patricia Hill Collins suggests that African American mothers often socialize their female children _____.
    a.   to be subordinate to men
    b.   to be dominant over men
    c.   to perform traditional sex roles
    d.   to be critical

44. Male peer groups place more pressure on boys to do "masculine" things than female peer groups place on girls to do "female" things. For example, girls are allowed to wear jeans and play soccer, but boys are not allowed to wear dresses and play hopscotch with the girls. This illustrates the cultural message that masculine activities and behavior are _____.
    a.   more important than feminine activities and behavior
    b.   not as important as feminine activities and behavior
    c.   more complex than feminine activities and behavior
    d.   less complex than feminine activities and behavior

45. Which of the following is probably the strongest influence on adolescent boys' development of gender identity?
    a.   parents
    b.   clergy
    c.   peers
    d.   teachers

46. Social research suggests that virtually all schools intentionally or unintentionally show favoritism toward boys over girls. This pattern of actions is known as _____.
    a.   gender relations
    b.   sexual hierarchy
    c.   sexual preference
    d.   gender bias

47. Studies suggest that the _____ of girls is affected in a negative way by lack of attention from teachers, sexual harassment by male peers, stereotyping of females in textbooks, and biased tests.
    a.   body image
    b.   self-esteem
    c.   verbal ability
    d.   marriageability

48. Women are more likely than men to _____.
    a.   earn an undergraduate college degree
    b.   get high GPAs in college
    c.   earn a graduate degree
    d.   (1 and 2 only)

49. Men are more likely than women to choose a college major in which of the following subjects?
    a.   chemistry, biology, or physics
    b.   computer technology
    c.   architecture
    d.   (all of the above)

50. Gender socialization _____ as women and men complete their training or education and join the work force.
    a.   virtually ceases
    b.   begins to decline in influence
    c.   reverses itself
    d.   continues

51. According to feminist scholars, women experience _____ as a result of economic, political, and educational discrimination.
    a.   sexual orientation
    b.   gender inequality
    c.   empowerment
    d.   pay equity

52. _____ refers to the concentration of women and men in different occupations, jobs, and places of work. In 1997, for example, 98 percent of all secretaries in the United States were women.
    a.   Gender bias
    b.   Sexual orientation
    c.   Heterogeneity
    d.   Gender segregation

53. In 1997, _____ percent of all U.S. engineers were men.
    a.   38
    b.   58
    c.   78
    d.   98

54. Women are _____ at the top executive levels of U.S. corporations.
    a.   well represented
    b.   not represented
    c.   under represented
    d.   represented in proportion to the percentage of women in the U.S. population

55. Occupational segregation contributes to a _____, which is the disparity between women's and men's earnings.
    a. salary increment
    b. salary potential
    c. pay gap
    d. pay increment

56. The _____ is calculated by dividing women's earning by men's to yield a percentage, also known as the earnings ratio.
    a. salary increment
    b. salary potential
    c. pay gap
    d. pay increment

57. White women in 1998 earned _____ percent as much as white men.
    a. 28
    b. 48
    c. 68
    d. 88

58. African American women earned _____ of what white male workers earned in 1998.
    a. 28
    b. 48
    c. 68
    d. 88

59. Latinas earned _____ percent of what white male workers earned in 1998.
    a. 29
    b. 39
    c. 49
    d. 59

60. Women's earnings tend to _____ when they reach their late 30s and early 40s.
    a. decrease
    b. stay the same
    c. increase
    d. be equal to men's earnings

61. Men's earnings tend to _____ as they age.
    a. decrease
    b. stay the same
    c. increase
    d. be equal to women's earnings

62. Pay equity, also known as _____ is the belief that wages ought to reflect the worth of a job, not the gender or race of the worker.
    a. gender equity
    b. comparable worth
    c. sexual worth
    d. gender equality

63. For every dollar earned by men in the occupations of bookkeeper, computer programmer, cook, lawyer, office manager, and social worker, women earned _____ cents or less.
    a. 20
    b. 40
    c. 60
    d. 80

64. In jobs that employ mostly women, such as nursing, secretarial work, and elementary teaching, _____.
    a. women earn less than the men in these occupations
    b. men earn less than men in male-dominated occupations
    c. women earn less than women in male-dominated occupations
    d. (all of the above)

65. According to sociologist Arlie Hochschild, women who work outside the home usually do the greater share of home household tasks as well. Hochschild refers to this as the "double day" or the _____.
    a. "second shift"
    b. "night shift"
    c. "swing shift"
    d. "graveyard shift"

66. According to the _____ theoretical perspective, male domination causes all forms of human oppression, including racism and classism.
    a. conflict
    b. liberal feminist
    c. radical feminist
    d. functionalist

67. According to the _____ theoretical perspective, women's roles as nurturers and care givers are very important in contemporary industrialized societies.
    a. conflict
    b. liberal feminist
    c. radical feminist
    d. functionalist

68. According to the _____ theoretical perspective, what individuals earn is the result of their own choices (the kinds of training, education, and experience they accumulate, for example) and of the labor market need (demand) and availability (supply) of certain kinds of workers at specific points in time.
    a. conflict
    b. human capital
    c. radical feminist
    d. functionalist

69. According to the _____ theoretical perspective, the gendered division of labor results from males having more economic, physical, political, and interpersonal power than women.
    a. conflict
    b. human capital
    c. neoclassical economic
    d. functionalist

70. _____ is the belief that women and men are equal and should be valued equally and have equal rights.
    a. The Bill of Rights
    b. Comparable worth
    c. Feminism
    d. Sexism

71. Persons who hold to the _____ theoretical perspective believe that the roots of women's oppression lie in women's lack of equal civil rights and education opportunities.
    a. conflict
    b. liberal feminist
    c. radical feminist
    d. functionalist

72. Persons who hold to the _____ theoretical perspective argue that for women's condition to improve, patriarchy must be abolished.
    a. functionalist
    b. neoclassical economic
    c. human capital
    d. radical feminist

73. According to advocates of the _____ theoretical perspective, the only way to achieve gender equality is to eliminate capitalism and develop a socialist economy that would bring equal pay and rights to women.
    a. functionalist
    b. neoclassical economic
    c. human capital
    d. socialist feminist

74. Psychologist Aida Hurtada suggests that distinctive differences exist between the world views of white (non-Latina) women who participate in the women's movement and many Chicanas, who have a strong sense of identity with their own communities. Hurtada's approach is best described as _____.
    a. functionalism
    b. human capital theory
    c. multicultural feminism
    d. socialist feminism

75. Overall, women earn approximately _____ cents on the dollar compared with men.
    a. 37
    b. 47
    c. 67
    d. 77

True-False Questions

1. Thinness has always been the "ideal" body image for women, throughout human history.

2. According to your textbook, most people have an accurate perception of their physical appearance.

3. Having engaged in a homosexual act means that the person is homosexual in their sexual orientation.

4. A person's sex is determined by what sex they were biologically born as.

5. A person's gender is socially determined.

6. Genital mutilation of girls and women is practiced in more than 25 countries of the world.

7. More than one-fourth of all U.S. children live with their mother only, as compared with just 5 percent who reside with their father only.

8. Gender-appropriate behavior is learned through the socialization process.

9. Research has shown that very little of a child's gender socialization is due to the influence of parents.

10. Studies show that teachers treat girls and boys differently in the classroom.

11. College instructors pay more attention to men than to women in their classes.

12. The mass media are a powerful source of gender socialization.

13. The workplace is an example of a gendered social institution.

14. Job segregation by gender is primarily due to the individual abilities of workers, and their different motivations and material needs.

15. On the average, women's wages are always lower than men's, no matter what their age.

Chapter 10: Answers to Practice Test Questions

(question-answer-page)

Multiple Choice Questions

1. d 280	41. c 296	6. T 294
2. d 284	42. b 296	7. T 295
3. d 284	43. d 296	8. T 295
4. b 284	44. a 297	9. F 296
5. a 285	45. c 297	10. T 298
6. d 285	46. d 298	11. T 299
7. a 286	47. b 298	12. T 300
8. b 286	48. d 299	13. T 302
9. d 286	49. d 299	14. F 303
10. b 286	50. d 300	15. T 304
11. a 286	51. b 302	
12. d 286	52. d 302	
13. a 286	53. d 302	
14. b 287	54. c 302	
15. b 287	55. c 303	
16. c 287	56. c 303	
17. c 287	57. c 305	
18. d 287	58. b 305	
19. c 287	59. b 305	
20. d 288	60. a 305	
21. b 289	61. c 305	
22. a 288	62. b 305	
23. b 289	63. d 305	
24. c 289	64. d 305	
25. d 289	65. a 306	
26. d 290	66. c 309	
27. b 290	67. d 306	
28. c 290	68. b 307	
29. b 290	69. a 308	
30. a 290	70. c 308	
31. b 290	71. b 308	
32. c 291	72. d 309	
33. d 291	73. d 310	
34. c 291	74. c 310	
35. d 291	75. d 311	
36. b 291		
37. a 292	**True-False Questions**	
38. d 293	1. F 286	
39. d 294	2. F 286	
40. d 295	3. F 287	
	4. T 290	
	5. T 290	

Chapter 11
Families and Intimate Relationships

Multiple Choice Questions

1. Sociologists view family-related issues such as divorce and child care as _____.
    a. personal problems requiring microlevel solutions
    b. social concerns requiring macrolevel solutions
    c. personal problems requiring macrolevel solutions
    d. social concerns requiring microlevel solutions

2. A _____ is a relationship in which people live together with commitment, form an economic unit and care for any young, and consider their identity to be significantly attached to the group.
    a. cohort
    b. family
    c. secondary group
    d. culture

3. Census data show that the marriage rate has _____ in the United States since 1960.
    a. gone down by about two-thirds
    b. gone down by about one-third
    c. stayed about the same
    d. increased by about one-third

4. About _____ percent of U.S. family households are composed of a married couple with one or more children under age eighteen.
    a. 6
    b. 26
    c. 46
    d. 76

5. _____ refers to a social network of people based on common ancestry, marriage or adoption.
    a. Genealogy
    b. Heredity
    c. Kinship
    d. Homogamy

6. In preindustrial societies, the primary form of social organization is through _____ ties.
    a. occupational
    b. kinship
    c. organizational
    d. secular

7. Recent studies have shown that adult children of divorced parents are _____ to dissolve their own marriages than they were two decades ago.
    a. less likely
    b. equally as likely
    c. more likely
    d. (there are not enough data to determine this)

8. The _____ is the family into which a person is born and in which early socialization usually takes place.
    a. family of procreation
    b. family of orientation
    c. kinship unit
    d. ancestry unit

9. The _____ is the family that a person forms by having or adopting children.
    a. family of procreation
    b. family of orientation
    c. kinship unit
    d. ancestry unit

10. Some sociologists have emphasized that traditional definitions of family do not encompass all types of contemporary families. For example, many gay men and lesbians have _____.
    a. "families we choose"
    b. "families of organization"
    c. "pseudo-families"
    d. "families of blood ties"

11. Persons in nontraditional family structures may include those with blood ties and legal ties, but it may also include _____, which are those who are not actually related by blood but who are accepted as family members.
    a. optional kin
    b. fictive kin
    c. honorary members
    d. acting members

12. A(n) _____ is a family unit composed of relatives in addition to parents and children who live in the same household.
    a. nuclear family
    b. adoptive family
    c. generation
    d. extended family

13. A(n) _____ is a family composed of one or two parents and their dependent children, all of whom live apart from other relatives.
    a. nuclear family
    b. adoptive family
    c. generation
    d. extended family

14. Which of the following family types is typically the predominant family form in industrialized and urbanized societies?
    a. extended family
    b. nuclear family
    c. polygamous family
    d. horticultural family

15. Which of the following family types is typically the predominant family form in horticultural and agricultural societies?
    a. extended family
    b. nuclear family
    c. polygamous family
    d. egalitarian family

16. In the United States, about _____ percent of all households in 1998 were composed of a married couple with children under age eighteen, as compared with 31 percent in 1980.
    a. 25
    b. 40
    c. 55
    d. 70

17. _____ is a legally recognized and/or socially approved arrangement between two or more individuals that carries certain rights and obligations and usually involves sexual activity.
    a. Adoption
    b. Patrimony
    c. Cohabitation
    d. Marriage

18. In the United States, the only legally sanctioned form of marriage is _____.
    a. polygamy
    b. polyandry
    c. neolocal residence
    d. monogamy

19. Through a pattern of marriage, divorce, and remarriage, some people practice _____, a succession of marriages in which a person has several spouses over a lifetime but is legally married only one person at a time.
    a. annulment
    b. serial polygamy
    c. polyandry
    d. serial monogamy

20. _____ is the concurrent marriage of a man with two or more women.
    a. Polyandry
    b. Monogamy
    c. Serial monogamy
    d. Polygyny

21. _____ is the concurrent marriage of one woman with two or more men.
    a. Polyandry
    b. Monogamy
    c. Serial monogamy
    d. Polygyny

22. _____ is very rare; when it does occur, it is typically found in societies where men greatly outnumber women because of high rates of female infanticide.
    a. Polyandry
    b. Monogamy
    c. Serial monogamy
    d. Polygyny

23. Virtually all forms of marriage establish a system of descent so that kinship can be determined and inheritance rights established. _____ is a system of tracing descent through the father's side of the family.
    a. Matrilineal descent
    b. Patrilineal descent
    c. Bilateral descent
    d. Egalitarian descent

24. _____ is a system of tracing descent through the mother's side of the family.
    a. Matrilineal descent
    b. Patrilineal descent
    c. Bilateral descent
    d. Egalitarian descent

25. The most common form of kinship in industrial societies is _____.
    a. matrilineal descent
    b. patrilineal descent
    c. bilateral descent
    d. egalitarian descent

26. In systems of _____, inheritance of property and position is usually traced from the maternal uncle (mother's brother) to his nephew (mother's son).
   a. matrilineal descent
   b. patrilineal descent
   c. bilateral descent
   d. egalitarian descent

27. A(n) _____ family is a family structure in which authority is held by the eldest male (usually the father).
   a. matriarchal
   b. egalitarian
   c. traditional
   d. patriarchal

28. A(n) _____ family structure is one in which authority is held by the eldest female (usually the mother).
   a. matriarchal
   b. egalitarian
   c. traditional
   d. patriarchal

29. A(n) _____ family structure is one in which both partners share power and authority equally.
   a. matriarchal
   b. egalitarian
   c. traditional
   d. patriarchal

30. Although there has been a great deal of discussion about _____ families, scholars have found no historical evidence to indicate that true forms of this family type ever existed.
   a. matriarchal
   b. polygamous
   c. monogamous
   d. patriarchal

31. _____ residence refers to the custom of a married couple living in the same household (or community) as the husband's family.
   a. Patrilocal
   b. Matrilocal
   c. Neolocal
   d. Exogamous

32. _____ is the custom of a married couple living in the same household (or community) as the wife's parents.
  a. Patrilocal
  b. Matrilocal
  c. Neolocal
  d. Exogamous

33. Across the world's cultures, _____ residency is the most common form.
  a. patrilocal
  b. matrilocal
  c. neolocal
  d. exogamous

34. In industrialized nations such as the United States, most couples hope to live in a _____ residence, which is the custom of a married couple living in their own residence apart from both the husband's and the wife's parents.
  a. patrilocal
  b. matrilocal
  c. neolocal
  d. exogamous

35. People who marry people within their own social class, race/ethnicity, or religious affiliation are practicing _____.
  a. patrimony
  b. endogamy
  c. exogamy
  d. monogamy

36. People who marry people outside of their own social class, race/ethnicity, or religious affiliation are practicing _____.
  a. patrimony
  b. endogamy
  c. exogamy
  d. monogamy

37. According to the _____ theoretical perspective, families are sources of social inequality and conflict over values, goals, and access to resources and power.
  a. functionalist
  b. conflict
  c. symbolic interactionist
  d. postmodernist

38. According to the _____ theoretical perspective, the family is important in maintaining the stability of society and the well-being of individuals.
    a.   functionalist
    b.   conflict
    c.   symbolic interactionist
    d.   postmodernist

39. According to some _____ theorists, families in capitalist economies are similar to the work environment of a factory. Women are dominated by men in the home in the same manner that workers are dominated by capitalists and managers in factories.
    a.   functionalist
    b.   conflict
    c.   symbolic interactionist
    d.   postmodernist

40. Sociologist Jesse Bernard, writing from a _____ theory perspective, points out that women and men may experience marriage differently. Although the husband may see *his* marriage very positively, the wife may feel less positive about *her* marriage, and vice versa.
    a.   functionalist
    b.   conflict
    c.   symbolic interactionist
    d.   postmodernist

41. According to the _____ theoretical perspective, how family problems are perceived and defined depends on patterns of communication, the meanings people give to roles and events, and individuals' interpretations of family interactions.
    a.   functionalist
    b.   conflict
    c.   symbolic interactionist
    d.   postmodernist

42. Social scientist David Elkin, writing from a _____ theoretical perspective, describes the contemporary family as permeable--capable of being diffused or invaded in such a manner that an entity's original purpose is modified or changed. For example, the idea of romantic love may give way to the idea of consensual love, and the idea of maternal parenting may be transformed into a new idea of shared parenting.
    a.   functionalist
    b.   conflict
    c.   symbolic interactionist
    d.   postmodernist

43. According to the _____ theoretical perspective, families are diverse and fragmented. Boundaries between workplace and home are blurred.
a. functionalist
b. conflict
c. symbolic interactionist
d. postmodernist

44. In the United States, ideal culture emphasizes the importance of _____ as the basis for intimate relationships and establishment of families.
a. monetary considerations
b. kinship ties
c. religious teachings
d. romantic love

45. Kissing is viewed as positive in _____ cultures.
a. all of the world's
b. primarily Western
c. primarily African and Asian
d. primarily North American

46. According to the National Health and Social Life Survey (1994), _____ percent of American men reported that they have had at least one homosexual encounter resulting in orgasm.
a. 3
b. 9
c. 13
d. 23

47. Recently, some gay and lesbian activists have sought recognition of _____-- household partnerships in which an unmarried couple lives together in a committed, sexually intimate relationship and is granted the same rights and benefits as those accorded to married heterosexual couples.
a. pseudo-marriages
b. extended families
c. families of orientation
d. domestic partnerships

48. _____ refers to a couple who live together without being legally married.
a. Pseudo-marriage
b. Trial marriage
c. Cohabitation
d. Homogamy

49.   _____ refers to the pattern of individuals marrying those who have similar characteristics, such as race/ethnicity, religious background, age, education, or social class.
a.   Kinship
b.   Cohabitation
c.   Monogamy
d.   Homogamy

50.   Most people in the United States tend to choose marriage partners who are _____.
a.   different from themselves
b.   similar to themselves
c.   highly educated
d.   upper middle class

51.   Today, approximately _____ percent of all marriages in the United States are *dual-earner marriages*-- marriages in which both partners are in the labor force.
a.   30
b.   50
c.   70
d.   90

52.   Many married women leave their paid employment at the end of the day and go home to perform hours of housework and child care. Sociologist Arlie Hochschild refers to this as _____.
a.   double indemnity
b.   forced overtime
c.   the second shift
d.   the patriarchal secret

53.   On average, women in the United States are now having about _____ child(ren) each.
a.   1
b.   2
c.   3
d.   5

54.   *Infertility* is defined as an inability to conceive a child after a year of unprotected sexual relations. This condition affects nearly _____ U.S. couples, or one in twelve couples in which the wife is between the ages of fifteen and forty-four.
a.   1 million
b.   3 million
c.   5 million
d.   9 million

55. There is a _____ in the United States, which is a belief that having children is the norm and can be taken for granted, whereas those who choose not to have children believe they must justify their decision to others.
   a. childbirth bias
   b. nativity expectation
   c. kid rule
   d. pronatalist bias

56. Although there are thousands of children available for adoption in the United States, many prospective parents seek out children in developing nations because children who are available in the U.S. _____.
   a. may be sick
   b. are often nonwhite
   c. are sometimes seen as too old
   d. (all of the above)

57. For the approximately 6.4 million women who become pregnant each year in the United States, about _____ percent of pregnancies are unintended.
   a. 36
   b. 46
   c. 56
   d. 76

58. Unplanned pregnancies usually are the result of _____.
   a. lack of available contraceptives
   b. failure to use contraceptives
   c. lack of sex education
   d. involuntary sexual intercourse

59. _____ involves fertilizing a woman's eggs in a laboratory dish and then transferring them to the woman's womb.
   a. *In vitro* fertilization
   b. Endogamous fertilization
   c. Virgin birth
   d. Chemical fertilization

60. During the 1990s, the rate of teenage pregnancy (number of live births per 1,000 women age fifteen to nineteen) _____.
   a. declined
   b. remained the same
   c. increased
   d. (not enough data to determine this)

61. In recent years, the percentage of households that are headed by a single parent has
_____.
   a. declined
   b. remained the same
   c. increased
   d. (not enough data to determine this)

62. Which of the following groups exhibits the highest percentage of men who have never
married?
   a. African Americans
   b. Latinos
   c. whites
   d. (not enough data to determine this)

63. The category of the life course known as *childhood* is not viewed in the same way in
every type of society. The view of childhood as a time to attend school and learn the
necessary skills for the future, rather than perform unskilled labor, is most often seen in
_____ societies.
   a. agricultural
   b. horticultural
   c. hunting-and-gathering
   d. industrial

64. In preindustrialized societies, adolescents (teenagers) are viewed as _____.
   a. infants
   b. children
   c. adults
   d. delinquents

65. In industrialized societies, adolescents (teenagers) are viewed as _____.
   a. infants
   b. children
   c. adults
   d. neither children nor adults

66. In industrialized societies, the period of life known as *young adulthood* spans the period
of life approximately between adolescence and age _____.
   a. 29
   b. 34
   c. 39
   d. 44

67. What age span represents the period of the life course that sociologists refer to as *middle adulthood*?
   a. 30-45
   b. 35-50
   c. 40-65
   d. 45-60

68. The period of the life span known as *late adulthood* is generally considered to begin at age _____.
   a. 55
   b. 60
   c. 65
   d. 70

69. _____ refers to any intentional act or series of acts--whether physical, emotional, or sexual--that causes injury to a female or male spouse.
   a. Assault
   b. Aggravated assault
   c. Matrimonial battery
   d. Spouse abuse

70. Historically, individuals and law enforcement officials have adopted a policy of _____ in dealing with domestic violence.
   a. mandatory referral to social service agencies
   b. nonintervention
   c. frequent filing of lawsuits
   d. mandatory arrest of offenders

71. According to one study, approximately _____ percent of all older people are victims of elder abuse.
   a. 2
   b. 10
   c. 23
   d. 46

72. The divorce rate of Roman Catholics in the United States is about _____ that of Protestants.
   a. half
   b. equal to
   c. twice
   d. three times

73. Most Americans who divorce _____.
    a. do not remarry
    b. get remarried to someone who has not been married before
    c. get remarried to someone who has been divorced
    d. get remarried to someone who is from a different social class than themselves

74. In the 1990s, about _____ percent of all marriages were between previously married brides and/or grooms.
    a. 20
    b. 30
    c. 40
    d. 60

75. Which of the following categories of person is most likely to become remarried quickly after a divorce?
    a. women without children
    b. women with a college degree
    c. women with adult children
    d. women with less than a high school education

True-False Questions

1. Sexual expression is a necessary foundation of all families.

2. Adult children of divorced parents are more likely to dissolve their own marriages than they were two decades ago.

3. Studies have found that sexual activity is more satisfying to people who are in sustained relationships such as marriage, than to those who are not in such a relationship.

4. As societies evolve from horticultural and agricultural to industrialized and urbanized, the nuclear family becomes the predominant family form.

5. No society in human history has ever formally allowed the practice of *polygamy*.

6. The most prevalent pattern of power and authority in families is *patriarchy*.

7. According to French sociologist Emile Durkheim, one of the primary functions of the family is regulation of sexual behavior.

8. During the Industrial Revolution of the late 19th century, people came to view the public sphere of work (outside of the home) as primarily "women's work."

9.   According to the National Health and Social Life Survey (1994), approximately 2.8 percent of American men identify themselves as gay.

10. According to sociologist Arlie Hochschild, the unpaid housework that women do on the "second shift" amounts to an extra 6 months of work each year.

11. According to sociologist Charlene Miall, women who are involuntarily childless engage in "information management" to combat the social stigma associated with childlessness.

12. In the United States, fewer children are available for adoption today than in previous years, in part because better means of contraception exist.

13. Studies indicate that the United States has the lowest rate of teen pregnancy in the western industrialized world.

14. Research indicates that living in a one-parent family causes poor academic achievement, higher school absentee and dropout rates, more drug and alcohol abuse, and other problems.

15. According to sociologists, families are central to human existence.

Chapter 11: Answers to Practice Test Questions

(question-answer-page)

Multiple Choice Questions

1. b 316	41. c 325	6. T 321
2. b 316	42. d 324	7. T 323
3. b 317	43. d 325	8. F 325
4. b 317	44. d 326	9. T 326
5. c 317	45. b 326	10. F 328
6. b 317	46. b 326	11. T 329
7. a 317	47. d 326	12. T 330
8. b 318	48. c 327	13. F 331
9. a 318	49. d 327	14. F 332
10. a 319	50. b 327	15. T 333
11. b 319	51. b 327	
12. d 319	52. c 328	
13. a 319	53. b 329	
14. b 319	54. c 329	
15. a 319	55. d 329	
16. a 319	56. d 330	
17. d 320	57. c 330	
18. d 320	58. b 330	
19. d 320	59. a 330	
20. d 320	60. a 331	
21. a 320	61. c 332	
22. a 321	62. a 333	
23. b 321	63. d 334	
24. a 321	64. c 335	
25. c 321	65. d 335	
26. a 321	66. c 335	
27. d 321	67. c 335	
28. a 321	68. c 335	
29. b 321	69. d 336	
30. a 321	70. b 336	
31. a 321	71. a 338	
32. b 322	72. b 339	
33. a 322	73. c 339	
34. c 322	74. c 339	
35. b 322	75. d 340	
36. c 322		
37. b 323	**True-False Questions**	
38. a 322	1. F 316	
39. b 324	2. F 317	
40. c 324	3. T 317	
	4. T 319	
	5. F 320	

Chapter 12
Education and Religion

Multiple Choice Questions

1. In the "Scopes monkey trial," Tennessee substitute high school biology teacher John Scopes was found guilty of _____.
    a. sexual misconduct
    b. teaching about evolution
    c. teaching about religion
    d. stealing several monkeys

2. As a result of the Scopes trial, _____ remained illegal in Tennessee until 1967.
    a. sexual misconduct
    b. teaching about evolution
    c. teaching about religion
    d. stealing of monkeys

3. The doctrine of _____ is a belief in the divine origins of the universe and human beings based on a literal interpretation of the Bible.
    a. Evolutionism
    b. Literality
    c. Creationism
    d. Humanism

4. The American notion of separation of church and state is set forth in _____.
    a. the Bible
    b. the Bill of Rights
    c. the Declaration of Independence
    d. the original Constitution of the United States

5. Education and religion have in common the fact that they _____.
    a. are socializing institutions
    b. are mandatory for Americans
    c. are scientific
    d. teach about ethics and moral values

6. _____ is the subarea of sociology which primarily examines formal education or schooling in industrial societies.
    a. The sociology of formality
    b. The sociology of training
    c. The sociology of education
    d. Social theory

7.   _____ is the subarea of sociology which focuses on religious groups and organizations, on the behavior of individuals within those groups, and on ways in which religion is intertwined with other social institutions.
    a.   Sacred sociology
    b.   The sociology of spirituality
    c.   The sociology of creation
    d.   The sociology of religion

8.   About _____ percent of those age eighteen and over in the forty-eight contiguous states of the United States describe their religion as some Christian denomination.
    a.   46
    b.   66
    c.   86
    d.   96

9.   According to the _____ theoretical perspective, education contributes to the maintenance of society and provides people with an opportunity for self-enhancement and upward social mobility.
    a.   conflict
    b.   functionalist
    c.   symbolic interactionist
    d.   feminist

10.   According to the _____ theoretical perspective, education perpetuates social inequality and benefits the dominant class at the expense of all others.
    a.   conflict
    b.   functionalist
    c.   symbolic interactionist
    d.   latent functions

11.   According to Emile Durkheim, schools have the responsibility to teach _____.
    a.   religion
    b.   about inequality
    c.   moral values
    d.   computer skills

12.   Which of the following is a *manifest function* of education?
    a.   finding a marriage partner
    b.   creation of a generation gap
    c.   keeping students off the streets
    d.   production of new knowledge

13. Which of the following is a *latent function* of education?
    a. teaching academic subjects
    b. transmitting the culture to the next generation
    c. teaching cultural values
    d. matchmaking and production of social networks

14. Schools are responsible for teaching values such as discipline, respect, obedience, punctuality, and perserverance. This is a _____ of education.
    a. latent function
    b. latent trait
    c. manifest function
    d. manifest trait

15. Mandatory school attendance keeps students out of the full-time job market for a number of years, thus helping keep unemployment within reasonable bounds. This is a _____ of education.
    a. latent function
    b. latent trait
    c. manifest function
    d. manifest trait

16. Mathematics education in the United States does not compare favorably with that found in many other industrialized nations. This is an example of a _____ of education.
    a. cultural lag
    b. latent function
    c. manifest function
    d. dysfunction

17. According to the _____ theoretical perspective, schools perpetuate class, racial-ethnic, and gender inequalities in society as some groups seek to maintain their privileged position at the expense of others.
    a. functionalist
    b. conflict
    c. latent function
    d. manifest function

18. According to French sociologist Pierre Bourdieu, students have differing amounts of _____, which is social assets that include values, beliefs, attitudes, and competencies in language and culture.
    a. class reproduction
    b. cultural skills
    c. marriageable assets
    d. cultural capital

19. Middle- and upper-income parents endow their children with more _____ than do working-class and poverty-level parents.
    a. class dysfunctions
    b. cultural morality
    c. personality traits
    d. cultural capital

20. Proper attitudes toward education, socially approved dress and manners, and knowledge about books, art, music, and other forms of high and popular culture are examples of _____.
    a. class dysfunctions
    b. cultural morality
    c. personality traits
    d. cultural capital

21. Standardized tests that are used for grouping students by ability and for assigning students to classes often measure students' _____ rather than their "natural" intelligence or aptitude.
    a. class dysfunctions
    b. cultural morality
    c. personality traits
    d. cultural capital

22. In middle school, junior high, and high school, students often experience _____, which is the assignment of students to specific courses and education programs based on their test scores, previous grades, or both.
    a. discrimination
    b. prejudice
    c. tracking
    d. mainstreaming

23. Which of the following groups experience disadvantages because they are more frequently placed in the low tracks in specific subject areas, such as math and science, where they typically receive a lower quality of instruction?
    a. girls
    b. students of color
    c. low-income students
    d. (all of the above)

24. According to conflict theorists, the _____ is the transmission of cultural values and attitudes, such as conformity and obedience to authority, through implied demands found in rules, routines, and regulations of schools.
    a. *second shift*
    b. *open book*
    c. *dead end road*
    d. *hidden curriculum*

25. Some analysts suggest that parts of the _____, such as certain school symbols like war whoops, tomahawks, and mascots painted to look like "savages," may be offensive to Native Americans.
    a. *second shift*
    b. *open book*
    c. *dead end road*
    d. *hidden curriculum*

26. Educational attainment is extremely important in societies that emphasize _____, which is a process of social selection in which class advantage and social status are linked to the possession of academic qualifications.
    a. training
    b. credentialism
    c. lateral mobility
    d. socialization

27. A(n) _____ is a society in which persons who acquire the appropriate credentials for a job are assumed to have gained the position through what they know, not who they are or who they know.
    a. plutocracy
    b. bureaucracy
    c. oligarchy
    d. meritocracy

28. Conflict theorists point out that _____ is embedded in the formal and hidden curricula of schools.
    a. meritocracy
    b. gender bias
    c. feminism
    d. religion

29. The federal government provides _____ of the funding for the nation's elementary, junior high, and high schools.
    a. none
    b. little
    c. most
    d. all

30. Most of the funding for the nation's elementary, junior high, and high schools comes from _____.
    a. the federal income tax
    b. state legislative appropriations
    c. local property taxes
    d. (b and c only)

31. Schools have been segregated by race for most of the history of the United States. According to a recent study, racial segregation is _____ in U.S. schools.
    a. declining
    b. holding at about the same level
    c. increasing
    d. nonexistent

32. _____ is the abolition of legally sanctioned racial-ethnic segregation.
    a. Desegregation
    b. Integration
    c. Equality
    d. Busing

33. _____ is the implementation of specific action to change the racial-ethnic and/or class composition of the student body of a school.
    a. Desegregation
    b. Integration
    c. Equality
    d. Busing

34. Even after decades of effort toward desegregation and integration of schools, by 1995 _____ percent of the 24,000 students in Hartford, Connecticut public schools were African American or Latina/o.
    a. 33
    b. 53
    c. 73
    d. 93

35. Since 1980, the enrollment of low-income students in college has _____.
    a. declined
    b. remained about the same
    c. increased slightly
    d. greatly increased

36. The dropout rate for African American students is significantly higher than that for whites, a problem which scholars attribute to _____.
    a. race
    b. poverty
    c. inner-city living
    d. religion

37. Sociologists examining education from a _____ perspective may focus on classroom dynamics, examining the interpretations that students and teachers give to their interactions with one another.
    a. functionalist
    b. conflict
    c. symbolic interactionist
    d. human capital

38. According to sociologist Robert K. Merton, _____ is an unsubstantiated belief or prediction resulting in behavior that makes the originally false belief come true.
    a. a myth
    b. magic
    c. a superstition
    d. a self-fulfilling prophecy

39. If a teacher (as a result of stereotypes based on the relationship between IQ and race) believes that some students of color are less capable of learning, that teacher may treat them as if they were incapable of learning. This is an example of _____.
    a. a myth
    b. magic
    c. a superstition
    d. a self-fulfilling prophecy

40. According to the book *The Bell Curve* by Richard J. Herrnstein and Charles Murray (1994), intelligence is _____.
    a. the product of social factors
    b. genetically inherited
    c. higher in white Americans than in Asians
    d. higher in African Americans than in white Americans

41. The conclusions reached by authors Richard J. Herrnstein and Charles Murray in their book *The Bell Curve* _____.
    a. have been refuted by scholars
    b. have been supported by scholars
    c. have been ignored by scholars
    d. suggest that intelligence and race are not related

42. According to labeling theory, labeling certain minority students as *learning disabled* may result in _____.
    a. stigmatization
    b. a self-fulfilling prophecy
    c. tracking
    d. (all of the above)

43. A study in Ypsilanti, Michigan found that preschool programs such as Head Start had a(n) _____ impact on children.
   a. negative
   b. negligible
   c. positive
   d. uncertain

44. Some research suggests that girls receive subtle cues from adults that lead them to attribute success to _____ whereas boys learn to attribute success to _____.
   a. intelligence/ability, effort
   b. effort, intelligence/ability
   c. help from adults, help from peers
   d. help from peers, help from adults

45. Some analysts argue that girls may be the victim of _____, which is hostility or opposition toward persons assumed to have great mental ability or toward subject matter believed to necessitate significant intellectual ability or knowledge for its comprehension.
   a. gender literacy
   b. gender opposition
   c. anti-intellectualism
   d. anti-literacy

46. _____ is a system of beliefs, symbols, and rituals, based on some sacred or supernatural realm, that guides human behavior, gives meaning to life, and unites believers into a community.
   a. Magic
   b. Religion
   c. Superstition
   d. Astrology

47. According to sociologist Emile Durkheim, every culture sets certain things apart as _____, which means that they are set aside as extraordinary or supernatural.
   a. alien
   b. secular
   c. profane
   d. sacred

48. _____ refers to the everyday, secular, or "worldly" aspects of life.
   a. Alien
   b. Holy
   c. Profane
   d. Sacred

49. People often act out their religious beliefs in the form of _____, which are symbolic actions that represent religious meanings.
    a. superstitions
    b. rituals
    c. sects
    d. cults

50. Sociologist Randall Collins points out that "...saying prayers, singing a hymn, performing a primitive sacrifice or a dance, marching in a procession, kneeling before an idol or making the sign of the cross" are examples of _____.
    a. superstitions
    b. rituals
    c. sects
    d. cults

51. Which of the following categories of religion is *nontheistic*, because it does not focus on worship of a god or gods?
    a. simple supernaturalism
    b. transcendent idealism
    c. theism
    d. (a and b only)

52. Which of the following categories of religion is based on the belief that supernatural forces affect people's lives either positively or negatively?
    a. simple supernaturalism
    b. animism
    c. theism
    d. transcendent idealism

53. Which of the following categories of religion is the belief that plants, animals, or other elements of the natural world are endowed with spirits or life forces having an impact on events in society?
    a. simple supernaturalism
    b. animism
    c. theism
    d. transcendent idealism

54. Which of the following categories of religion is based on a belief in a god or gods?
    a. simple supernaturalism
    b. animism
    c. theism
    d. transcendent idealism

55.	_____ is a belief in a single, supreme being or god who is responsible for significant events such as the creation of the world.
	a.	Polytheism
	b.	Monotheism
	c.	Cult
	d.	Sect

56.	Which of the following categories of religion is identified with early hunting and gathering societies and with many Native American societies, in which everyday life was not separated from the elements of the natural world?
	a.	simple supernaturalism
	b.	animism
	c.	theism
	d.	transcendent idealism

57.	Which of the following major religions of the world is *monotheistic* in its beliefs?
	a.	Christianity
	b.	Judaism
	c.	Islam
	d.	(all of the above)

58.	Hinduism, Shinto, and a number of indigenous religions of Africa are forms of _____, which is a belief in more than one god.
	a.	Polytheism
	b.	Monotheism
	c.	Cult
	d.	Sect

59.	Each of the various Christian religions base their doctrines and practices on the teachings of _____.
	a.	Siddhartha Gautama
	b.	Muhammad
	c.	Abraham, Isaac, and Jacob
	d.	Jesus Christ

60.	The _____ theoretical perspective typically emphasizes ways in which religious beliefs and rituals can bind people together.
	a.	functionalist
	b.	conflict
	c.	symbolic interactionist
	d.	feminist

61. The _____ theoretical perspective focuses on the meanings that people give to religion in their everyday life.
    a.   functionalist
    b.   conflict
    c.   symbolic interactionist
    d.   feminist

62. The _____ theoretical perspective suggests that religion can be a source of false consciousness in society.
    a.   functionalist
    b.   conflict
    c.   symbolic interactionist
    d.   feminist

63. According to Emile Durkheim, religious beliefs and rituals are _____, which are group-held meanings that express something important about the group itself.
    a.   group meanings
    b.   collective representations
    c.   collective solidarities
    d.   group functions

64. Which of the following is NOT one of the three important functions of religions suggested by functionalists?
    a.   meaning and purpose
    b.   serving as an "opiate of the people"
    c.   social cohesion and a sense of belonging
    d.   social control and support for the government

65. _____ is the set of beliefs, rituals and symbols that makes sacred the values of the society and places the nation in the context of the ultimate system of meaning.
    a.   Christianity
    b.   Judaism
    c.   Civil religion
    d.   Secular religion

66. Which of the following theoretical perspectives sees religion as serving to justify the status quo and retard social change?
    a.   functionalist
    b.   conflict
    c.   symbolic interactionist
    d.   (all of the above)

67. Which of the following theoretical perspectives suggests that religion unites people under a "false consciousness," which is the belief that they share common interests with members of the dominant class?
   a. functionalist
   b. conflict
   c. symbolic interactionist
   d. (all of the above)

68. In his book *The Protestant Ethic and the Spirit of Capitalism (1976/1904-1905)*, _____ asserted that the religious teachings of John Calvin were directly related to the rise of capitalism
   a. Karl Marx
   b. Emile Durkheim
   c. Max Weber
   d. Daniel Patrick Moynihan

69. Which of the following theoretical approaches focuses on religion from a *microlevel* perspective?
   a. functionalist
   b. conflict
   c. symbolic interactionist
   d. (all of the above)

70. According to the _____ perspective, religion tends to promote conflict between groups and societies.
   a. functionalist
   b. conflict
   c. symbolic interactionist
   d. (none of the above)

71. According to feminist scholar Charlotte Perkins Gilman, religious thought and doctrine have always tended to be dominated by _____.
   a. bishops
   b. cardinals
   c. the middle class
   d. men

72. A(n) _____ is a religious organization that is so integrated into the dominant culture that it claims as its membership all members of a society.
   a. cult
   b. sect
   c. church
   d. ecclesia

73. A _____ is a large, bureaucratically organized religious organization that tends to seek accommodation with the larger society in order to maintain some degree of control over it.
    a. cult
    b. sect
    c. church
    d. ecclesia

74. A _____ is a religious group with practices and teachings outside the dominant cultural and religious traditions of a society.
    a. cult
    b. sect
    c. church
    d. ecclesia

75. A _____ is a relatively small religious group that has broken away from another religious organization to renew what it views as the original version of the faith.
    a. cult
    b. sect
    c. church
    d. ecclesia

True-False Questions

1. Functionalists argue that education contributes to the maintenance of society and provides people with an opportunity for self-enhancement and upward social mobility.

2. Transmission of the culture is a *latent function* of education.

3. Functionalists admit that U.S. education is not promoting the high-level skills in reading, writing, and mathematics that are needed in the global economy. This situation may be seen as a *dysfunction* of education.

4. According to research by sociologist Maureen T. Hallinan, girls are less likely than boys to move to a higher mathematics track in secondary schools.

5. School mascots and sports team names often perpetuate stereotypes of minority groups such as Native Americans.

6. Research using IQ scores has consistently found that white students are genetically smarter and better able to perform school tasks than are students of color.

7. Studies have found that labeling students as gifted can result in higher achievement levels by these students.

8. Crosses, altars, and holy books are examples of *sacred* objects.

9. In terms of numbers of members, the largest of the major world religions is Islam.

10. The primary sacred object of the United States' civil religion is the George Washington quarter-dollar coin.

11. According to the religious doctrine of *predestination*, God knows who will go to heaven and who will go to hell.

12. According to feminist scholar Charlotte Perkins Gilman, religious language has historically defined women as being nonexistent.

13. According to your textbook, all categories of religion require their members to have total commitment to the religious group.

14. Protestants constitute the largest religious body in the United States.

15. Some of the world's major religions started out as cults built around a charismatic leader.

Chapter 12: Answers to Practice Test Questions

(question-answer-page)

Multiple Choice Questions

1. b 344	40. b 355	4. T 350
2. b 344	41. a 355	5. T 351
3. c 344	42. d 355	6. F 355
4. b 344	43. c 355	7. T 355
5. a 345	44. b 356	8. T 356
6. c 345	45. c 356	9. F 358
7. d 345	46. b 356	10. F 360
8. c 346	47. d 356	11. T 361
9. b 346	48. c 356	12. T 362
10. a 347	49. b 356	13. F 363
11. c 347	50. b 356	14. T 366
12. d 347	51. b 357	15. T 368
13. d 348	52. a 357	
14. c 349	53. b 357	
15. a 349	54. c 357	
16. d 349	55. b 357	
17. b 349	56. b 357	
18. d 349	57. d 357	
19. d 349	58. a 357	
20. d 349	59. d 358	
21. d 350	60. a 359	
22. c 350	61. c 359	
23. d 351	62. b 359	
24. d 350	63. b 359	
25. d 351	64. b 359	
26. b 351	65. c 360	
27. d 351	66. b 360	
28. b 351	67. b 361	
29. b 351	68. c 361	
30. d 352	69. c 362	
31. c 352	70. b 352	
32. a 352	71. d 363	
33. b 352	72. d 363	
34. d 352	73. c 363	
35. a 353	74. a 365	
36. b 353	75. b 364	
37. c 353		
38. d 353	**True-False Questions**	
39. d 353	1. T 346	
	2. F 347	
	3. T 349	

Chapter 13
Politics and the Economy in Global Perspective

Multiple Choice Questions

1. In the case of *Wilson v. Layne*, the U.S. Supreme Court ruled that _____.
    a. laws limiting the terms of elected officials are unconstitutional
    b. police cannot search locked vehicles without a warrant
    c. U.S. citizens cannot sue U.S. corporations in foreign courts
    d. media representatives cannot photograph suspects during "ride-alongs"

2. _____ is the social institution through which power is acquired and exercised by some people and groups.
    a. Economics
    b. Politics
    c. The military
    d. Government

3. _____ is the formal organization that has the legal and political authority to regulate the relationships among members of a society and between the society and those outside its borders.
    a. Economics
    b. Politics
    c. The military
    d. Government

4. _____ is the political entity that possesses a legitimate monopoly over the use of force within its territory to achieve its goals.
    a. The State
    b. The economy
    c. The military
    d. Society

5. _____ focuses on the social circumstances of politics and explores how the political arena and its actors are intertwined with social institutions such as the economy, religion, education, and the media.
    a. Political sociology
    b. Political science
    c. Econometrics
    d. Political economics

6. According to your textbook, the essence of politics is _____.
    a. elections
    b. legislation
    c. interest groups
    d. power

7. _____ is the ability of persons or groups to achieve their goals despite opposition from others.
   a.   Influence
   b.   Persuasiveness
   c.   Power
   d.   Charisma

8. Political leaders seek to legitimize their power by turning it into _____, which is power that people accept as legitimate rather than coercive.
   a.   a constitution
   b.   legislation
   c.   authority
   d.   democracy

9. According to sociologist G. William Domhoff, the media tend to reflect the biases of which of the following groups?
   a.   influential people and groups
   b.   the powerless
   c.   the middle class
   d.   women and minorities

10. The most basic form of power is _____.
   a.   higher education
   b.   physical force
   c.   money and financial resources
   d.   laws and the criminal justice system

11. According to Max Weber's classification of ideal types of authority, _____ is power legitimized by law or written rules and regulations.
   a.   traditional authority
   b.   charismatic authority
   c.   rational-legal authority
   d.   (none of the above)

12. According to Max Weber's classification of ideal types of authority, _____ is power that is legitimized on the basis of long-standing custom.
   a.   traditional authority
   b.   charismatic authority
   c.   rational-legal authority
   d.   (none of the above)

13. According to Max Weber's classification of ideal types of authority, _____ is power that is legitimized on the basis of a leader's exceptional personal qualities or the demonstration of extraordinary insight and accomplishment that inspires loyalty and obedience from followers.
   a. traditional authority
   b. charismatic authority
   c. rational-legal authority
   d. (none of the above)

14. _____ tends to be temporary and relatively unstable because it derives primarily from individual leaders and a group of faithful followers.
   a. Traditional authority
   b. Charismatic authority
   c. Rational-legal authority
   d. (none of the above)

15. _____ occur(s) when charismatic authority is succeeded by a bureaucracy controlled by a rationally established authority or by a combination of traditional and bureaucratic authority.
   a. Traditional authority
   b. Routinization of charisma
   c. Rational-legal authority
   d. Primary groups

16. Rational-legal authority, also known as _____, is based on an organizational structure that includes a clearly defined division of labor, hierarchy of authority, formal rules, and impersonality.
   a. primary authority
   b. secondary authority
   c. monarchy
   d. bureaucracy

17. _____ is held by elected or appointed government officials and by officers in a formal organization. However, authority is invested in the *office*, not in the *person* who holds the office.
   a. Traditional authority
   b. Routinization of charisma
   c. Rational-legal authority
   d. Secondary authority

18. Napoleon, Adolf Hitler, Dr. Martin Luther King, Jr., César Chávez and Mother Theresa illustrate Max Weber's concept of _____.
   a. traditional authority
   b. charismatic authority
   c. rational-legal authority
   d. (none of the above)

19. Four main types of political systems are found in nation-states. _____ is a political system controlled by rulers who deny popular participation in government.
   a.   Monarchy
   b.   Authoritarianism
   c.   Totalitarianism
   d.   Democracy

20. Four main types of political systems are found in nation-states. _____ is a political system in which power resides in one person or family and is passed from generation to generation through lines of inheritance.
   a.   Monarchy
   b.   Authoritarianism
   c.   Totalitarianism
   d.   Democracy

21. Four main types of political systems are found in nation-states. _____ is a political system in which the people hold the ruling power either directly or through elected representatives.
   a.   Monarchy
   b.   Authoritarianism
   c.   Totalitarianism
   d.   Democracy

22. Four main types of political systems are found in nation-states. _____ is a political system in which the state seeks to regulate all aspects of people's public and private lives.
   a.   Monarchy
   b.   Authoritarianism
   c.   Totalitarianism
   d.   Democracy

23. The nations of Great Britain, Sweden, Spain, and Netherlands illustrate the type of political system known as _____.
   a.   monarchy
   b.   authoritarianism
   c.   totalitarianism
   d.   democracy

24. The National Socialist (Nazi) party in Germany during World War II is an example of the type of political system known as _____. During the Nazi era, military leaders sought to control all aspects of national life, not just government operations.
   a.   monarchy
   b.   authoritarianism
   c.   totalitarianism
   d.   democracy

25. _____ is a type of democratic political system in which citizens meet together regularly to debate and decide the issues of the day.
    a.   Representative democracy
    b.   Pluralist democracy
    c.   Direct Participatory democracy
    d.   *demos kratein*

26. _____ is a type of democratic political system in which citizens elect persons to convey their concerns and interests, and the government is expected to be responsive to the wishes of the people.
    a.   Representative democracy
    b.   Pluralist democracy
    c.   Direct Participatory democracy
    d.   *demos kratein*

27. Even though the United States has a democratic political system, women were denied the right to vote until passage of the Nineteenth Amendment to the Constitution in _____.
    a.   1814
    b.   1865
    c.   1920
    d.   1945

28. According to the _____ model, power in political systems is widely dispersed throughout many competing interest groups.
    a.   symbolic interactionist
    b.   elite
    c.   pluralist
    d.   competition

29. According to the _____ model, power in political systems is concentrated in the hands of a small group of wealthy and politically powerful persons, and the masses are relatively powerless.
    a.   symbolic interactionist
    b.   elite
    c.   pluralist
    d.   consensus

30. _____ are political coalitions made up of individuals or groups that share a specific interest they wish to protect or advance with the help of the political system.
    a.   Cohorts
    b.   Special interest groups
    c.   Populations
    d.   Professional standards groups

31. Labor unions such as the AFL-CIO, and public interest or citizens' groups such as the American Conservative Union and Zero Population Growth are examples of _____.
    a. cohorts
    b. special interest groups
    c. populations
    d. professional standards groups

32. _____ are sometimes referred to as *pressure groups* (because they put pressure on political leaders) or *lobbies*.
    a. Cohorts
    b. Special interest groups
    c. Populations
    d. Professional standards groups

33. _____ are organizations of special interest groups that solicit contributions from donors and fund campaigns to help elect (or defeat) candidates based on their stances on specific issues.
    a. Labor unions
    b. Denominations
    c. Interest Funding Campaigns
    d. Political Action Committees

34. Which of the following groups is not usually represented by PACs?
    a. ideological interest groups
    b. public interest groups
    c. large corporations
    d. Medicare recipients

35. Ben Nighthorse Campbell is a United States Senator and also a _____.
    a. descendant of African American slaves
    b. tobacco company PAC
    c. Latino
    d. Cheyenne chief

36. According to _____ theorists, government exists for the benefit of wealthy or politically powerful elites who use the government to impose their will on the masses.
    a. conflict
    b. functionalist
    c. symbolic interactionist
    d. consensus

37. According to the _____ model, power is highly concentrated at the top of a pyramid-shaped social hierarchy, and public policy reflects the values and preferences of the elite, not the preferences of the people.
    a. functionalist
    b. consensus
    c. equality
    d. elite

38. Sociologist C. Wright Mills referred to the leaders at the top of business, the executive branch of the federal government, and the military as _____.
    a. the trilateral commission
    b. the chosen few
    c. the power elite
    d. the military/industrial complex

39. Sociologist G. William Domhoff uses the term _____ to signify a relatively fixed group of privileged people who wield sufficient power to constrain political processes and serve underlying capitalist interests.
    a. the chosen few
    b. the power elite
    c. the military/industrial complex
    d. the ruling class

40. A _____ is an organization whose purpose is to gain and hold legitimate control of government: it is usually composed of people with similar attitudes, interests, and socioeconomic status.
    a. political action committee
    b. labor union
    c. political party
    d. party caucus

41. According to your textbook, the Republican and Democratic parties are _____, which means that they are dominated by active elites who hold views that are further from the center of the political spectrum than are those of a majority of members of their party.
    a. dictatorships
    b. monarchies
    c. oligarchies
    d. conglomerates

42. _____ is the process by which people learn political attitudes, values, and behavior.
    a. Political learning
    b. Political socialization
    c. Government learning
    d. Electoral socialization

43. On the average, _____ of the voting-age population has voted in nonpresidential elections over the past thirty years.
    a. less than one-quarter
    b. less than one-half
    c. more than two-thirds
    d. more than three-quarters

44. According to the U.S. Bureau of the Census, about _____ percent of the voting-age population (age 18 and older) voted in the 1996 presidential election.
    a. 28.9
    b. 48.9
    c. 68.9
    d. 88.9

45. About _____ percent of the top-echelon positions in the federal government are held by white men.
    a. 30
    b. 50
    c. 70
    d. 90

46. The *Iron Triangle*, also referred to as _____, is the mutual interdependence of the military establishment and private military contractors.
    a. the Bermuda Triangle
    b. the military-industrial complex
    c. strange bedfellows
    d. Devil's pact

47. The _____ is the social institution that ensures the maintenance of society through the production, distribution, and consumption of goods and services.
    a. government
    b. Congress
    c. criminal justice system
    d. economy

48. In preindustrial societies, most workers engage in _____, which is the extraction of raw materials and natural resources from the environment.
    a. surplus labor
    b. primary sector production
    c. secondary sector production
    d. capitalism

49. In industrial economies, most workers engage in _____, which is the processing of raw materials (from the primary sector) into finished goods.
    a. surplus labor
    b. primary sector production
    c. secondary sector production
    d. interdependence

50. A *postindustrial economy* is based on _____, which is the provision of services rather than goods.
    a. primary sector production
    b. secondary sector production
    c. tertiary sector production
    d. postindustrial operations

51. Fast-food service, transportation, communication, education, real estate, advertising, sports, and entertainment are examples of _____.
    a. primary sector production
    b. secondary sector production
    c. tertiary sector production
    d. postindustrial operations

52. _____ is an economic system characterized by private ownership of the means of production, from which personal profits can be derived through market competition and without governmental intervention.
    a. Capitalism
    b. Communism
    c. Socialism
    d. Totalitarianism

53. _____ is based on the right of individuals to own income-producing property.
    a. Capitalism
    b. Communism
    c. Socialism
    d. Totalitarianism

54. _____ are large-scale organizations that have legal powers, such as the ability to enter into contracts and buy and sell property, separate from their individual owners.
    a. Cults
    b. Sects
    c. Enterprises
    d. Corporations

55. _____ are large corporations that are headquartered in one country but sell and produce goods and services in many countries.
   a. Free-trade enterprises
   b. Firms
   c. Transnational corporations
   d. Secondary-market corporations

56. A(n) _____ is said to exist when several companies overwhelmingly control an entire industry.
   a. complete monopoly
   b. adjusted monopoly
   c. oligopoly
   d. oligarchy

57. A(n) _____ exists when four or fewer companies supply 50 percent or more of a particular market.
   a. shared monopoly
   b. adjusted monopoly
   c. oligopoly
   d. oligarchy

58. The "Big Three" U.S. automobile companies, and U.S. cereal companies (three of which control 77 percent of the market) are examples of _____.
   a. shared monopolies
   b. adjusted monopolies
   c. oligopolies
   d. oligarchies

59. Corporations with control both within and across industries are often formed by a series of mergers and acquisitions across industries. These corporations are referred to as _____.
   a. companies
   b. partnerships
   c. conglomerates
   d. multinationals

60. _____ are combinations of businesses in different commercial areas, all of which are owned by one holding company.
   a. Companies
   b. Partnerships
   c. Conglomerates
   d. Multinationals

61. The Clayton Antitrust Act of 1914 made which of the following situations or actions illegal?
    a.   one person sitting on two or more corporate boards of directors at the same time
    b.   one person simultaneously sitting on the boards of two corporations that directly compete with each other
    c.   a U.S. citizen sitting on the board of corporations with headquarters outside of the U.S.
    d.   one person sitting on the board of directors of both a bank and a corporation that borrows from that bank

62. According to your textbook, which of the following situations occurs as a result of interlocking corporate directorships?
    a.   increased competition among corporations
    b.   decreased competition among corporations
    c.   less cooperation among corporations
    d.   less financial success by corporations

63. The doctrine of *laissez-faire* (also known as *market economy* or *free enterprise*), assumes that capitalism works best when _____.
    a.   it is unregulated
    b.   it is strictly regulated by the government
    c.   monopolies are declared to be illegal
    d.   excessive profits are not allowed

64. _____ is an economic system characterized by public ownership of the means of production, the pursuit of collective goals, and centralized decision making.
    a.   Capitalism
    b.   Socialism
    c.   Democracy
    d.   Monarchy

65. According to Karl Marx, communism is characterized by _____.
    a.   individual ownership of private property
    b.   common ownership of all economic resources
    c.   authoritarian and dictatorial governments
    d.   shared monopolies

66. Most social scientists agree that the term _____ includes most doctors, natural scientists, engineers, computer scientists, certified public accountants, economists, social scientists, psychotherapists, lawyers, policy experts of various kinds, professors, some journalists and editors, some clergy, and some artists and writers.
    a.   *power elite*
    b.   *occupational group*
    c.   *professionals*
    d.   *wage workers*

67. Which of the following is NOT one of the five major characteristics of a profession that are discussed in the textbook?
   a. autonomy
   b. government regulation
   c. authority
   d. altruism (concern for others)

68. Sociologists distinguish between employment in two types of labor market. The _____ consists of low-paying jobs with few benefits and very little job security or possibility for future advancement.
   a. service labor market
   b. primary labor market
   c. secondary labor market
   d. blue-collar labor market

69. Sociologists refer to the number of workers a manager supervises as his or her _____.
   a. control index
   b. span of control
   c. circle of influence
   d. span of hierarchy

70. _____ is part-time work, temporary work, or subcontracted work that offers advantages to employers but that can be detrimental to the welfare of workers.
   a. Primary labor
   b. Service work
   c. Incentive-based employment
   d. Contingent work

71. Which of the following practices came about as a result of the efforts of U.S. labor unions?
   a. the 8-hour workday
   b. the 5-day work week
   c. health and retirement benefits
   d. (all of the above)

72. Today, approximately _____ percent of all U.S. employees belong to a labor union.
   a. 7
   b. 17
   c. 37
   d. 67

73. Since the 1960s, the *proportion* of all employees who are labor union members has
_____.
  a. decreased
  b. remained about the same
  c. slightly increased
  d. increased sharply

74. Politics and the economy are so intertwined in the United States and on a global basis that many social scientists speak of the two as a single entity, the _____.
  a. *global economy*
  b. *global village*
  c. *political economy*
  d. *politico/economic conglomerate*

75. Some analysts see the political and economic future of the world as a(n) _____, which consists of information technologies such as the Internet and World Wide Web coming together to change economic relationships and the way in which politics and government are conducted.
  a. digital democracy
  b. information democracy
  c. linked institution
  d. cyberspace government

True-False Questions

1. *Authority* is power that people accept as legitimate rather than coercive.

2. According to Max Weber, *charismatic authority* is power that is legitimized on the basis of long-standing custom.

3. Approximately 35 *nation-states* currently exist throughout the world.

4. In *constitutional monarchies*, the royalty serve as symbolic rulers or heads of state while actual authority is held by elected officials in national parliaments.

5. The Internet, the World Wide Web, and all-news channels such as CNN and MSNBC make it much more difficult for contemporary authoritarian and totalitarian governments to control the flow of information the world receives about their activities.

6. According to the pluralist model, power in political systems is widely dispersed throughout many competing interest groups.

7. People who are paid to influence legislation on behalf of specific clients are referred to as *lobbyists*.

8.   In recent years, politicians have relied less and less on money from political action committees (PACs).

9.   According to sociologist G. William Domhoff, the *ruling class* consists of approximately the top 15 percent of the U.S. population.

10.   The Democratic and Republican political parties have dominated the U.S. political system since the Civil War.

11.   The United States has one of the highest percentages of voter turnout of all Western nations.

12.   Postindustrial economies are based on the provision of goods rather than services.

13.   The Microsoft Corporation has been the subject of federal investigations and lawsuits because it so dominates certain areas of the computer software industry that it has virtually no competitors in those areas.

14.   *Interlocking corporate directorates* are illegal under United States law.

15.   One of the primary attributes of a profession is higher education.

Chapter 13: Answers to Practice Test Questions

(question-answer-page)

Multiple Choice Questions

1. d 371
2. b 372
3. d 372
4. a 372
5. a 372
6. d 372
7. c 372
8. c 373
9. a 373
10. b 373
11. c 375
12. a 375
13. b 375
14. b 375
15. b 375
16. d 375
17. c 375
18. b 376
19. b 377
20. a 377
21. d 377
22. c 378
23. a 377
24. c 378
25. c 378
26. a 378
27. c 379
28. c 379
29. b 381
30. b 379
31. b 379
32. b 380
33. d 380
34. d 381
35. d 380
36. a 381
37. d 381
38. c 381
39. d 381
40. c 382

41. c 383
42. b 383
43. b 384
44. b 384
45. d 384
46. b 386
47. d 386
48. b 387
49. c 387
50. c 387
51. c 387
52. a 387
53. a 388
54. d 388
55. c 388
56. c 389
57. a 389
58. a 389
59. c 390
60. c 390
61. b 390
62. b 390
63. a 391
64. b 391
65. b 392
66. c 393
67. b 393
68. c 395
69. b 395
70. d 396
71. d 397
72. b 397
73. a 397
74. c 399
75. a 400

True-False Questions

1. T 373
2. F 375
3. F 376
4. T 377
5. T 378
6. T 379
7. T 380
8. F 381
9. F 381
10. T 382
11. F 384
12. F 387
13. T 389
14. F 390
15. T 394

Chapter 14
Health, Health Care, and Disability

Multiple Choice Questions

1.   The World Health Organization defines *health* as _____.
        a.   the absence of disease
        b.   complete physical, mental, and social well-being
        c.   a sense of physical wellness
        d.   strictly a biological phenomenon

2.   According to the World Health Organization, health includes _____ factors.
        a.   physical
        b.   social
        c.   psychological
        d.   (all of the above)

3.   Illness is _____.
        a.   strictly a biological phenomenon
        b.   the same from culture to culture
        c.   socially defined
        d.   the same in all historical time periods

4.   _____ is an institutionalized system for the scientific diagnosis, treatment, and prevention of illness.
        a.   Life expectancy
        b.   Demedicalization
        c.   Social epidemiology
        d.   Medicine

5.   The number of people infected with HIV/AIDS _____ between 1990 and 1997.
        a.   dropped by half
        b.   remained about the same
        c.   more than doubled
        d.   increased by a factor of 4

6.   _____ refers to an estimate of the average lifetime of people born in a specific year.
        a.   The demographic transition
        b.   Demography
        c.   The infant mortality rate
        d.   Life expectancy

7.   In the low-income nation of Zambia, approximately _____ percent of the people are not expected to live to age 60.
      a.   20
      b.   40
      c.   60
      d.   80

8.   United Nations data show that the infant mortality rate in high-income nations is _____ the infant mortality rate in low-income nations.
      a.   sharply lower than
      b.   about the same as
      c.   slightly higher than
      d.   sharply higher than

9.   According to the World Health Organization, about five million babies born in low-income countries during 1998 died during _____ of life.
      a.   the first month
      b.   the first six months
      c.   the first year
      d.   the first three years

10.   During the past 15 years, life expectancy at birth has risen to more than 70 years in 84 countries, up from _____ countries in 1990.
      a.   15
      b.   25
      c.   35
      d.   55

11.   During the past 15 years, life expectancy in low-income nations has increased on average from 53 to _____ years.
      a.   55
      b.   62
      c.   67
      d.   72

12.   The United States spends the equivalent of _____ per person on health care each year.
      a. $351
      b. $3,510
      c. $35,010
      d. $350,010

13. Sweden spends less per person on health care each year than does the United States. Average life expectancy in Sweden is _____ the average life expectancy in the U.S.
    a.   lower than
    b.   about the same as
    c.   higher than
    d.   (no data are available to determine this)

14. _____ is the study of the causes and distribution of health, disease, and impairment throughout a population.
    a.   Medicine
    b.   Health care
    c.   Population demography
    d.   Social Epidemiology

15. Rates of illness are highest among which of the following groups?
    a.   the very young
    b.   the middle-aged
    c.   the very old
    d.   (a and c)

16. _____ are illnesses that are long term or lifelong and that develop gradually or are present from birth.
    a.   Acute diseases
    b.   Chronic diseases
    c.   Ascribed conditions
    d.   Achieved conditions

17. _____ are illnesses that strike suddenly and cause dramatic incapacitation and sometimes death.
    a.   Acute diseases
    b.   Chronic diseases
    c.   Ascribed conditions
    d.   Achieved conditions

18. Which of the following is/are closely linked to chronic diseases and premature death?
    a.   tobacco and alcohol
    b.   coffee consumption
    c.   low-fat diets
    d.   consumption of vitamin supplements

19. The life expectancy of women in the United States is _____ the life expectancy of U.S. men.
    a.   lower than
    b.   about the same as
    c.   higher than
    d.   (no data available)

20. _____ are any substances--other than food and water--that, when taken into the body, alter its functioning in some way.
    a. Vitamins
    b. Supplements
    c. Nourishers
    d. Drugs

21. When a person takes a drug for a specific purpose such as reducing a fever or controlling a cough, this is known as _____ use.
    a. therapeutic
    b. recreational
    c. controlled
    d. administered

22. When a person takes a drug for the purpose of achieving a pleasurable feeling or psychological state, this is known as _____ use.
    a. therapeutic
    b. recreational
    c. instrumental
    d. secondary

23. Alcohol and tobacco are _____.
    a. primarily used for recreational purposes
    b. illegal if used by persons under a certain age
    c. dangerous if used to excess
    d. (all of the above)

24. Which of the following beverages has the highest annual rate of consumption by U.S. adults?
    a. coffee
    b. milk
    c. alcohol
    d. tea

25. The average American adult consumes approximately _____ of beer per year.
    a. 3.2 quarts
    b. 3.2 gallons
    c. 32 gallons
    d. 320 gallons

26. The average American adult consumes approximately _____ of wine per year.
    a. 2.5 quarts
    b. 2.5 gallons
    c. 25 gallons
    d. 250 gallons

27. The average American adult consumes approximately _____ of liquor per year.
    a.   1.8 quarts
    b.   1.8 gallons
    c.   18 gallons
    d.   180 gallons

28. Which of the following conditions have been shown to result from chronic, heavy drinking or alcoholism?
    a.   nutritional deficiencies
    b.   cardiovascular problems
    c.   cirrhosis of the liver
    d.   (all of the above)

29. Which of the following is the most widely-used illegal drug in the United States?
    a.   marijuana
    b.   cocaine
    c.   heroin
    d.   vitamin supplements

30. About _____ of U.S. people over the age of 12 have tried marijuana at least once.
    a.   one-quarter
    b.   one-third
    c.   one-half
    d.   two-thirds

31. Among which of the following age groups is marijuana use most common in the United States?
    a.   12-17
    b.   18-25
    c.   26-35
    d.   36-50

32. The acronym STD stands for _____.
    a.   standard treatment diagnoses
    b.   standard treatment developments
    c.   sexually-transmitted disabilities
    d.   sexually-transmitted diseases

33. AIDS was first identified in the U.S. in _____.
    a.   1961
    b.   1971
    c.   1981
    d.   1991

34. Worldwide, the number of persons with AIDS or HIV is _____.
    a. decreasing sharply
    b. remaining about the same
    c. increasingly slightly
    d. increasing sharply

35. Worldwide, children account for about _____ percent of AIDS deaths each year.
    a. 10
    b. 20
    c. 30
    d. 40

36. Over the past several decades, the incidence of heart disease and some types of cancer has _____ in the United States.
    a. decreased
    b. remained about the same
    c. increased
    d. (no data are available)

37. In 1910, the Carnegie Foundation--at the request of the American Medical Association--conducted an exhaustive study of U.S. medical schools. Results of the study are known as _____.
    a. the Carnegie report
    b. the Flexner report
    c. the AMA survey
    d. the Carnegie survey of medical training

38. Throughout its history, medical care in the U.S. has been provided on a(n) _____ basis.
    a. income fund reimbursable
    b. fee-for-service
    c. insurance company reimbursement
    d. health maintenance organization (HMO)

39. Which of the following is one of the new advances in medicine that is discussed in your textbook?
    a. pharmacist's assistants
    b. plasma-assisted surgery
    c. increased academic requirements for physicians
    d. use of robots in surgery

40. *Bloodless surgery* refers to operations that _____.
    a. do not require making incisions in the skin of the patient
    b. recycle the patient's blood during surgery
    c. are performed to the exterior of the patient's body
    d. do not require blood transfusions

41. Between 1960 and 1997, the cost per person of U.S. medical care increased by more than
    _____.
    a. 5 times
    b. 15 times
    c. 25 times
    d. 45 times

42. According to medical sociologist Paul Starr, the main reason that the cost of U.S. medical care increased sharply beginning in the 1960s is _____.
    a. third-party fee-for-service
    b. third-party socialized medicine
    c. a decline in the role of medical insurance programs
    d. increased competition among physicians

43. _____ is the nationwide public health insurance program that provides medical care for U.S. residents who are covered by social security or who are eligible and "buy into" the program by paying a monthly premium.
    a. Medicaid
    b. Medicare
    c. FICA
    d. Blue Cross/Blue Shield

44. _____ is the nationwide public health insurance program that was established to make health care more available to the poor.
    a. Medicaid
    b. Medicare
    c. FICA
    d. Blue Cross/Blue Shield

45. _____ are designed to provide, for a set monthly fee, total care with an emphasis on prevention to avoid costly treatment later.
    a. Fee-for-service providers
    b. Health Maintenance Organizations (HMOs)
    c. Medical care cooperatives
    d. Fitness centers

46. Another approach to controlling health care costs in the U.S. is _____, which is any system of cost containment that closely monitors and controls health care providers' decisions about medical procedures, diagnostic tests, and other services that should be provided to patients.
    a. fee-for-service
    b. fitness centers
    c. managed care
    d. monitored medicine

47. Under _____ programs, physicians must get approval before they perform certain procedures or admit a patient to a hospital.
   a. fee-for-service
   b. fitness center
   c. managed care
   d. monitored medicine

48. About _____ of all U.S. citizens are without health insurance or had difficulty getting or paying for medical care at some time in the last year.
   a. one-quarter
   b. one-third
   c. one-half
   d. two-thirds

49. In contrast to the United States, Canada has a system of _____, in which all citizens receive medical services paid for by tax revenues.
   a. fee-for-service medicine
   b. socialized medicine
   c. universal health care
   d. mandatory hospitalization

50. _____ is a health care system in which the government owns the medical care facilities and employs the physicians.
   a. Fee-for-service medicine
   b. Socialized medicine
   c. Universal health care
   d. Mandatory hospitalization

51. The medical care system in Great Britain is a _____ system.
   a. fee-for-service medicine
   b. socialized medicine
   c. universal health care
   d. mandatory hospitalization

52. In order to increase the number of health care providers after the 1949 revolution in the populous nation of China, a large number of persons with little or no formal training were assigned to provide medical care under the supervision of trained physicians. These persons were known as _____.
   a. physician extenders
   b. street doctors
   c. barefoot doctors
   d. (all of the above)

53.	Which of the following is NOT one of the social implications of advanced medical technology discussed in the textbook?
    a.	creates options that alter human relationships
    b.	increases the cost of medical care
    c.	raises provocative questions about the nature of human life
    d.	discourages use of documents such as the *living will*

54.	One alternative to traditional medicine is _____, which is an approach to health care that focuses on prevention of illness and disease and is aimed at treating the whole person (body and mind) rather than just the part or parts in which symptoms occur.
    a.	faith healing
    b.	holistic medicine
    c.	chiropractic care
    d.	deductive medicine

55.	Which of the following is a form of alternative medicine?
    a.	chiropractic
    b.	spiritual healing
    c.	massage therapy
    d.	(all of the above)

56.	According to the textbook, the medical establishment is opposed to _____.
    a.	methods of healing
    b.	the pharmaceutical industry
    c.	nonscientific methods
    d.	scientific methods

57.	According to the _____ theoretical approach, sickness may be viewed as a deviant behavior.
    a.	functionalist
    b.	conflict
    c.	symbolic interactionist
    d.	feminist

58.	Sociologist Talcott Parsons referred to *the set of patterned expectations that defines the norms and values appropriate for individuals who are sick and for those who interact with them* as _____.
    a.	the hospital mindset
    b.	the medical role
    c.	the sick role
    d.	the sick status

59. According to Talcott Parsons, persons who assume _____ are showing others that they are not responsible for their condition, and that they are temporarily exempt from their normal roles and obligations.
   a. the hospital mindset
   b. the medical role
   c. the sick role
   d. the sick status

60. According to functionalist theorist Talcott Parsons, illness is _____.
   a. functional for society
   b. dysfunctional for society
   c. evidence of power differences between groups
   d. an illusion

61. Sociologists who adopt a _____ theoretical approach examine how race, class, and gender inequalities affect health and health care.
   a. functionalist
   b. conflict
   c. symbolic interactionist
   d. postmodern

62. Persons who do not earn enough to afford private medical care, but who earn just enough money to keep them from qualifying for Medicaid are referred to in the textbook as _____.
   a. the medically indigent
   b. medically disadvantaged
   c. the uninsurable
   d. health care victims

63. _____ encompasses both local physicans and hospitals as well as global health-related industries such as insurance companies and pharmaceutical and medical supply companies.
   a. The military-industrial complex
   b. The medical-industrial complex
   c. The health care alliance
   d. The pharmaceutical triangle

64. According to the _____ theoretical perspective, illness is a social construction.
   a. functionalist
   b. conflict
   c. symbolic interactionist
   d. postmodern

65. Scholars who adopt a _____ theoretical perspective point out that victims of illness such as AIDS are often blamed for their fate, and stigmatized as a result.
   a.   functionalist
   b.   conflict
   c.   symbolic interactionist
   d.   postmodern

66. _____ refers to the process whereby nonmedical problems become defined and treated as illnesses or disorders.
   a.   Treatment
   b.   Therapy
   c.   Medical definition
   d.   Medicalization

67. Symbolic interactionist theorists note that defining practices such as gambling as a psychological illness ("compulsive gambling") allows physicians to determine what is "normal" and "acceptable" behavior. This process is known as _____.
   a.   medical definition
   b.   psychological definition
   c.   medicalization of deviance
   d.   psychological deviance

68. The American Psychiatric Association has removed homosexuality from its list of mental disorders. This process of removal is referred to by sociologists as _____.
   a.   medicalization of deviance
   b.   demedicalization
   c.   psychiatric removal
   d.   demystification

69. According to the _____ theoretical perspective, health and illness cannot be strictly determined by medical criteria. They are social constructions as well.
   a.   functionalist
   b.   conflict
   c.   symbolic interactionist
   d.   feminist

70. Writing from a _____ perspective, Michel Foucault suggests that truth in medicine--like all other areas of life--is a social construction.
   a.   functionalist
   b.   conflict
   c.   feminist
   d.   postmodern

71. _____ refers to a reduced ability to perform tasks one would normally do at a given stage of life and that may result in stigmatization or discrimination against the person.
    a. Deviance
    b. Disability
    c. Discrimination
    d. Disease

72. Most disabilities in the U.S. result from _____.
    a. accidents
    b. disease
    c. war
    d. (all of the above)

73. According to Patrisha Wright, a spokesperson for the Disability Rights Education and Defense Fund, "...You can become disabled from your mother's poor nutrition or from falling off your polo pony." Wright's statement refers to the importance of _____ in causing disability.
    a. age
    b. geographic location
    c. race/ethnicity
    d. social class

74. Disabilities that are present from a person's birth are referred to as _____.
    a. innate
    b. congenital
    c. proscriptive
    d. marginal

75. People with disabilities are often the object of _____.
    a. prejudice
    b. discrimination
    c. stigmatization
    d. (all of the above)

True-False Questions

1. Women are more likely than men to make use of the health care system in the United States.

2. Men at all ages have lower rates of fatal diseases than women.

3. According to your textbook, race is a more influential determinant of health and mortality than social class is.

4.   Nicotine, the active drug in tobacco, has been shown to be more addictive than heroin.

5.   Overall, the percentage of the U.S. population who smoke has increased since the 1964 Surgeon General's warning.

6.   The illegal drug that is used more than any other in the United States is cocaine.

7.   Untreated syphillis can cause cardiovascular problems, brain damage, or death.

8.   At present, there is no known cure for genital herpes, there is only treatment for the symptoms of the disease.

9.   Since 1995, the number of U.S. deaths due to AIDS has shown an increasing trend.

10.   Medical researchers have discovered that the HIV virus can be spread by casual contact such as shaking hands.

11.   During the 19th century, one of the ways that people became medical doctors was by purchasing a mail-order diploma.

12.   The U.S. system of medical care has been described as a two-tier system, with one standard of care for those who can afford it, and another standard of care for the poor.

13.   Federal law requires all hospitals and other medical facilities to honor the terms of a living will.

14.   According to theorists who adopt a radical conflict theory approach, the only way to reduce inequalities in the U.S. health care structure is to eliminate capitalism or curb the medical-industrial complex.

15.   African Americans have lower rates of disability than whites.

Chapter 14: Answers to Practice Test Questions

(question-answer-page)

Multiple Choice Questions

1. b 404
2. d 405
3. c 405
4. d 405
5. c 405
6. d 405
7. d 407
8. a 407
9. a 407
10. d 407
11. b 407
12. b 407
13. c 408
14. d 408
15. d 408
16. b 408
17. a 408
18. a 408
19. c 408
20. d 409
21. a 409
22. b 409
23. d 409
24. c 409
25. c 409
26. b 409
27. b 409
28. d 409
29. a 410
30. b 410
31. b 410
32. d 410
33. c 411
34. d 411
35. b 412
36. a 412
37. b 412
38. b 413
39. d 413
40. d 413

41. c 414
42. a 414
43. b 415
44. a 415
45. b 415
46. c 416
47. c 416
48. b 417
49. c 417
50. b 417
51. b 418
52. d 419
53. d 419
54. b 420
55. d 421
56. c 421
57. a 421
58. c 421
59. c 421
60. b 421
61. b 422
62. a 423
63. b 422
64. c 423
65. c 423
66. d 423
67. c 424
68. b 424
69. c 424
70. d 425
71. b 425
72. d 426
73. d 426
74. b 426
75. d 428

True-False Questions

1. T 408
2. F 409
3. F 409
4. T 410
5. F 410

6. F 410
7. T 411
8. T 411
9. F 411
10. F 412
11. T 412
12. T 414
13. T 420
14. T 423
15. F 426

Chapter 15
Population and Urbanization

Multiple Choice Questions

1. The world's population reached _____ people in 1999.
    a. 6 million
    b. 60 million
    c. 6 billion
    d. 60 billion

2. The world's population is increasing by approximately _____ people per year.
    a. 9.4 million
    b. 94 million
    c. 940 million
    d. 9 billion

3. _____ is a subfield of sociology that examines population size, composition, and distribution.
    a. Census taking
    b. Demography
    c. Democracy
    d. Political economics

4. A(n) _____ is a group of people who live in a specified geographic area.
    a. cohort
    b. aggregate
    c. sample
    d. population

5. Changes in population occur as a result of _____.
    a. fertility
    b. mortality
    c. migration
    d. (all of the above)

6. _____ is the actual level of childbearing for an individual or a population.
    a. Fertility
    b. Mortality
    c. Migration
    d. Demography

7. The primary biological factor affecting _____ is the number of women of childbearing age.
   a. fertility
   b. mortality
   c. migration
   d. demography

8. Sociologists usually consider _____ to be the childbearing age of women.
   a. 11-35
   b. 15-45
   c. 18-40
   d. 18-45

9. Social factors influencing _____ include the roles available to women in a society and prevalent viewpoints regarding what constitutes the "ideal" family size.
   a. fertility
   b. mortality
   c. migration
   d. demography

10. Based on biological capacity alone, most women could produce _____ children during their childbearing years.
    a. about 6
    b. about 12
    c. about 15
    d. 20 or more

11. _____ is the potential number of children who could be born if every woman reproduced at her maximum biological capacity.
    a. Fertility
    b. Fecundity
    c. Population capacity
    d. Demographic potential

12. Which of the following factors tend to limit fertility?
    a. infanticide
    b. contraception
    c. sterilization
    d. (all of the above)

13. The basic measure of fertility is the _____, which is the number of live births per 1,000 people in a population in a given year.
    a. crude birth rate
    b. corrected birth rate
    c. population rate
    d. demographic rate

14. The all-time highest levels of fertility in the U.S. were seen during which time period?
    a. during World War I
    b. during the 1930s
    c. after World War II
    d. after the Vietnam War

15. In most areas of the world, women are having _____ children than in past years.
    a. fewer
    b. about the same number of
    c. slightly more
    d. sharply more

16. The primary cause of world population growth in recent years has been _____.
    a. greater fertility
    b. reduced mortality
    c. the need for more effective contraceptives
    d. people's ignorance of sexual matters

17. The *crude death rate* is the simplest measure of _____.
    a. fertility
    b. mortality
    c. population capacity
    d. demographic potential

18. Which of the following diseases has been virtually eliminated in high-income, developed nations?
    a. malaria
    b. polio
    c. tetanus
    d. (all of the above)

19. Many serious diseases have been virtually eliminated in high-income, developed nations as a result of _____.
    a. improved sanitation
    b. improved personal hygiene
    c. vaccinations
    d. (all of the above)

20. According to the United Nations, about _____ children under age 15 are infected with AIDS each day worldwide.
    a. 16
    b. 160
    c. 1,600
    d. 16,000

21.	_____ is defined as the number of deaths of infants under 1 year of age per 1,000 live births.
	a.	The fertility rate
	b.	The crude death rate
	c.	The infant mortality rate
	d.	The child death rate

22.	For persons born in the United States in 1999, life expectancy at birth was _____ years.
	a.	69.2
	b.	74.2
	c.	76.2
	d.	80.2

23.	The life expectancy of persons born in the United States in 1999 is _____ the life expectancy of persons born in Japan in 1999.
	a.	lower than
	b.	the same as
	c.	slightly higher than
	d.	much higher than

24.	Life expectancy for African American males is about _____ years, as compared to 74.2 years for white males.
	a.	54.6
	b.	64.6
	c.	70.6
	d.	78.6

25.	_____ is the movement of people from one geographic area to another for the purpose of changing residency.
	a.	Fertility
	b.	Mortality
	c.	Migration
	d.	Demography

26.	_____ is the number of people living in a specific geographic area.
	a.	Density
	b.	Distribution
	c.	Immigration
	d.	Emigration

27.	_____ refers to the physical location of people throughout a geographic area.
	a.	Density
	b.	Distribution
	c.	Immigration
	d.	Emigration

28. Immigration and emigration are two types of _____.
   a. population density
   b. mortality
   c. migration
   d. demography

29. In the 1800s, about 5 percent of the U.S. population resided in urban areas; by 1998, about _____ percent did so.
   a. 20
   b. 40
   c. 60
   d. 80

30. Which of the following is an example of *involuntary migration* or *forced migration*?
   a. slavery
   b. Jews fleeing Nazi Germany
   c. Haitians fleeing the Cedras regime in the 1990s
   d. (all of the above)

31. _____ refers to the biological and social characteristics of a population.
   a. Population density
   b. Population distribution
   c. Population composition
   d. Population migration

32. Age, sex, race, marital status, education, occupation, income, and size of household are part of _____.
   a. population density
   b. population distribution
   c. population composition
   d. population migration

33. The _____ is defined as the number of males for every hundred females in a given population.
   a. gender ratio
   b. male ratio
   c. sex ratio
   d. female ratio

34. A _____ of 100 indicates an equal number of males and females in the population.
   a. gender ratio
   b. male ratio
   c. sex ratio
   d. female ratio

35. In the 25-44 year age category, and in all older groups, there are _____ women than men in the United States.
   a. fewer
   b. about the same number of
   c. more
   d. (no data available)

36. By age 65, there are about _____ men for every 100 women in the U.S.
   a. 30
   b. 70
   c. 110
   d. 130

37. A _____ is a graphic representation of the distribution of a population by age and sex.
   a. demographic chart
   b. population chart
   c. population pyramid
   d. demographic funnel

38. Scholars predict that the world's population will reach _____ by 2050.
   a. 60 million
   b. 800 million
   c. 10 billion
   d. 200 billion

39. According to Thomas Malthus, the population, if left unchecked, will always _____.
   a. outgrow the geographic area in which it lives
   b. exceed the amount of available natural resources, such as oil
   c. develop new means of contraception
   d. exceed the food supply

40. According to Thomas Malthus, human populations, if left unchecked, tend to increase in a(n) _____ fashion.
   a. arithmetic
   b. geometric
   c. exponential
   d. (b and c only)

41. According to Thomas Malthus, food supplies tend to increase in a(n) _____ fashion.
   a. arithmetic
   b. geometric
   c. exponential
   d. (b and c only)

42. According to Thomas Malthus, mortality risks such as famine, disease, and war are _____ on population.
    a. positive checks
    b. negative checks
    c. preventive checks
    d. moral restraints

43. According to Thomas Malthus, *moral restraint* is _____.
    a. a preventive check
    b. not possible
    c. a mortality risk
    d. a doubling factor

44. According to Karl Marx and Friedrich Engels, overpopulation occurs because _____.
    a. of food surpluses
    b. capitalists need a ready supply of poor workers
    c. there has been a revolution to overthrow capitalism
    d. of lack of sexual restraint

45. Advocates of the _____ perspective view the Earth as a "dying planet" with too many people and too little food, compounded by environmental degradation.
    a. Demographic transition
    b. Neo-Malthusian
    c. Neo-Functionalist
    d. Conflict

46. The highest incidences of AIDS have occurred on which continent?
    a. North America
    b. South America
    c. Asia
    d. Africa

47. Some people have only one or two children in order to bring about _____, which is the point at which no population increase occurs from year to year.
    a. gender equality
    b. population composition
    c. zero population growth
    d. demographic transition

48.   _____ is the process by which some societies have moved from high birth and death rates to relatively low birth and death rates as a result of technological development.
   a.   Fertility
   b.   Fecundity
   c.   Population composition
   d.   Demographic transition

49.   In the African nation of Botswana, _____ percent of all persons between ages 15 and 49 are infected with HIV.
   a.   6
   b.   16
   c.   36
   d.   56

50.   According to Demographic Transition theory, birth rates and death rates are high in _____ societies.
   a.   preindustrial
   b.   early industrial
   c.   advanced industrial and urban
   d.   postindustrial

51.   According to Demographic Transition theory, birth rates and death rates are low in _____ societies.
   a.   preindustrial
   b.   early industrial
   c.   advanced industrial and urban
   d.   (all of the above)

52.   According to Demographic Transition theory, birth rates are high and death rates are declining in _____ societies.
   a.   preindustrial
   b.   early industrial
   c.   advanced industrial and urban
   d.   (all of the above)

53.   Current estimates suggest that the world population is increasing about _____ percent per year.
   a.   0.8
   b.   1.8
   c.   18
   d.   180

54. The number of births required to replace deaths over an extended period is referred to as _____.
   a. population leveling
   b. replacement level
   c. mortality level
   d. fertility level

55. _____ is a subfield of sociology that examines social relationships and political and economic structures in the city.
   a. Demography
   b. Population dynamics
   c. Urban sociology
   d. Sociology of cities

56. About 3 percent of the world's population lived in cities two hundred years, ago, as compared with almost _____ percent today.
   a. 10
   b. 30
   c. 50
   d. 70

57. _____ is the process by which an increasing proportion of a population lives in cities rather than in rural areas.
   a. Urban sociology
   b. Suburbanization
   c. Demographic transition
   d. Urbanization

58. According to sociologist Gideon Sjoberg, which of the following is a necessary precondition that must be present in order for cities to develop?
   a. a favorable physical environment
   b. an advanced technology (for the era)
   c. a well-developed social organization
   d. (all of the above)

59. Scholars disagree over when the earliest cities developed. However, estimates generally place the origin of cities to between 3,500 and _____ years B.C.E.
   a. 4,000
   b. 8,000
   c. 15,000
   d. 40,000

60. The largest preindustrial city was _____, which may have had a population of 650,000 by 100 C.E.
    a. Athens
    b. Rome
    c. Sparta
    d. Constantinople

61. Ferdinand Tönnies described _____ as a society in which social relationships are based on personal bonds of friendship and kinship and on intergenerational stability, such that people have a commitment to the entire group and feel a sense of togetherness.
    a. *Gemeinschaft*
    b. *Gesellschaft*
    c. the metropolis
    d. the concentric zones

62. Ferdinand Tönnies described _____ as a society that exhibits impersonal and specialized relationships, with little long-term commitment to the group or consensus on values.
    a. *Gemeinschaft*
    b. *Gesellschaft*
    c. the rural area
    d. the concentric zones

63. New York City became the United States' first _____, which is defined as one or more central cities and their surrounding suburbs that dominate the economic and cultural life of a region.
    a. *Gemeinschaft*
    b. *Gesellschaft*
    c. metropolis
    d. regional city

64. According to author Randy Shilts, AIDS was spread across the continents of the world _____.
    a. by mail
    b. by air travel
    c. by ship
    d. by wind currents

65. According to Emile Durkheim, _____ is characterized by interdependence based on the elaborate division of labor found in large, urban societies.
    a. mechanical solidarity
    b. organic solidarity
    c. anomie
    d. altruism

66. According to Emile Durkheim, _____ is characterized by a simple division of labor and shared religious beliefs such as are found in small, agrarian societies.
    a. mechanical solidarity
    b. organic solidarity
    c. anomie
    d. altruism

67. University of Chicago sociologist Robert Park (1915) based his analysis of the city on _____, which is the study of the relationship between people and their physical environment.
    a. conflict theory
    b. human ecology
    c. human genetics
    d. postmodern theory

68. Sociologist Ernest W. Burgess (1925) developed the _____ model, an ideal construct that attempted to explain why some cities expand radially from a central business core.
    a. central cities
    b. concentric zones
    c. inner city decay
    d. suburban

69. According to Ernest W. Burgess's model, _____ is the process by which a new category of people or type of land use arrives in an area previously occupied by another group or type of land use.
    a. succession
    b. invasion
    c. immigration
    d. gentrification

70. _____ is the process by which members of the middle and upper-middle classes, especially whites, move into the central-city area and renovate existing properties.
    a. Succession
    b. Invasion
    c. Immigration
    d. Gentrification

71. According to Homer Hoyt's _____ model (1939), residences of a particular type and value tend to grow outward from the center of the city in wedge-shaped sectors.
    a. concentric zone
    b. sector
    c. multiple nuclei
    d. public patriarchy

72. According to Chauncey Harris and Edward Ullman's _____ model (1945), cities do not have one center from which all growth radiates, but rather have numerous centers of development based on specific urban needs or activities.
   a. concentric zone
   b. sector
   c. multiple nuclei
   d. public patriarchy

73. _____ theorists argue that cities grow as a result of land use and urban development decisions intended to benefit some groups at the expense of others.
   a. Functionalist
   b. Conflict
   c. Symbolic interactionist
   d. Ecological

74. According to feminist scholar Lynn M. Appleton, different kinds of cities have different _____, which are prevailing ideologies of how women and men should think, feel, and act; how social positions and control of resources should be managed; and how relationships between men and women should be conducted.
   a. social structures
   b. gender regimes
   c. sex ratios
   d. sex rules

75. According to sociologist Immanuel Wallerstein, nations may be divided into _____ tiers.
   a. one
   b. two
   c. three
   d. four

True-False Questions

1. Scholars estimate that more people will die of AIDS in the United States than have died in all of the wars fought by this nation.

2. Fertility rates are always higher than fecundity rates.

3. According to the World Health Organization, only about 25 percent of people infected with AIDS worldwide were infected through heterosexual relations.

4. Persons who are HIV-positive are more likely to live in cities than in rural areas.

5. According to your textbook, life expectancy varies by race.

6. The population pyramids of all nations are nearly identical.

7. According to Karl Marx and Friedrich Engels, it is technologically possible to produce enough food and other goods needed to meet the demands of a growing population.

8. It is estimated that about 1000 African children will ultimately be left without a mother because of the AIDS epidemic.

9. Postindustrial cities are dominated by "light" industry, such as software manufacturing; information-processing services, educational complexes, and medical centers.

10. Symbolic interactionists examine the *experience* of city life.

11. Since World War II, a major population shift occurred in the United States as thousands of families moved from suburban areas to cities.

12. The 1990 census showed that about 20 percent of central-city residents were persons of color, although they constituted only 15.3 percent of the nation's population.

13. The practice whereby banks refuse to lend money for housing to persons from certain geographic areas is known as *scratching off*.

14. Disability rights advocates point out that structural barriers create a 'disabling" environment for many people, particularly in large, urban settings.

15. According to your textbook, rapid population growth is inevitable in the future.

Chapter 15: Answers to Practice Test Questions

(question-answer-page)

Multiple Choice Questions

1. c 434
2. b 434
3. b 435
4. d 435
5. d 435
6. a 435
7. a 435
8. b 435
9. a 435
10. d 435
11. b 435
12. d 435
13. a 437
14. c 437
15. a 437
16. b 437
17. b 437
18. d 437
19. d 437
20. c 437
21. c 437
22. c 438
23. a 438
24. b 438
25. c 438
26. a 438
27. b 438
28. c 438
29. d 438
30. d 439
31. c 439
32. c 439
33. c 439
34. c 439
35. c 439
36. b 439
37. c 439
38. c 441
39. d 441
40. d 441

41. a 441
42. a 441
43. a 441
44. b 441
45. b 442
46. d 442
47. c 442
48. d 442
49. c 443
50. a 442
51. c 442
52. b 442
53. b 444
54. b 444
55. c 445
56. c 445
57. d 445
58. d 445
59. b 445
60. b 446
61. a 446
62. b 446
63. c 447
64. b 447
65. b 448
66. a 448
67. b 448
68. b 448
69. b 448
70. d 449
71. b 449
72. c 450
73. b 450
74. b 451
75. c 452

True-False Questions

1. T 434
2. F 435
3. F 436
4. T 436
5. T 438

6. F 440
7. T 441
8. F 443
9. T 447
10. T 452
11. F 455
12. F 455
13. F 456
14. T 457
15. T 458

Chapter 16
Collective Behavior, Social Movements, and Social Change

Multiple Choice Questions

1. _____ is the alteration, modification, or transformation of public policy, culture, or social institutions over time.
    a. Social movements
    b. Social stratification
    c. Collective behavior
    d. Social change

2. In the 1970s, the federal government bought the homes in the Love Canal neighborhood of Niagara Falls, N.Y. and relocated the residents because _____.
    a. the homes were improperly constructed
    b. the residents were considered to be a security risk during the war years
    c. the homes had been built on a chemical dump site
    d. the residents had defaulted on their home mortgages

3. _____ is voluntary, often spontaneous activity that is engaged in by a large number of people and typically violates dominant group norms and values.
    a. Social movements
    b. Social stratification
    c. Collective Behavior
    d. Social Change

4. Unlike the *organizational behavior* found in corporations and voluntary associations, *collective behavior* lacks _____.
    a. an official division of labor
    b. a hierarchy of authority
    c. established rules and procedures
    d. (all of the above)

5. Crowds, mobs, riots, panics, fads, fashions, and public opinion are examples of _____.
    a. organizational behavior
    b. institutional behavior
    c. social movements
    d. collective behavior

6. A(n) _____ is a relatively large number of people who mutually transcend, bypass, or subvert established institutional patterns and structures.
    a. group
    b. cohort
    c. aggregate
    d. collectivity

7. Which of the following contributes to the likelihood that collective behavior will occur?
    a. structural factors that increase the chances of people responding in a particular way
    b. timing
    c. a breakdown in social control mechanisms
    d. (all of the above)

8. A common stimulus is an important factor in collective behavior. For example, Rachel Carson's book *Silent Spring*, which detailed the dangers of _____, led many people and groups to turn to activism.
    a. overpopulation
    b. pesticides
    c. nuclear war
    d. air pollution

9. People are more likely to engage in collective behavior in response to a common stimulus if _____.
    a. they are gathered together in one location
    b. they are physically separated from one another
    c. they act through "official channels"
    d. social control mechanisms are strong and effective

10. A(n) _____ is a relatively large number of people who are in one another's immediate vicinity.
    a. crowd
    b. mass
    c. institution
    d. society

11. A(n) _____ is a number of people who share an interest in a specific idea or issue but who are not in one another's immediate vicinity.
    a. crowd
    b. mass
    c. institution
    d. society

12. Social movements are more likely to flourish in which of the following types of society?
    a. totalitarian
    b. authoritarian
    c. socialist
    d. democratic

13.   Most sociologists believe that individuals act _____ when they are part of a crowd.
        a.   rationally
        b.   irrationally
        c.   without any regard to social norms
        d.   violently

14.   People in a shopping mall or a subway car are examples of _____.
        a.   conventional crowds
        b.   casual crowds
        c.   conventional aggregates
        d.   primary groups

15.   Religious services, graduation ceremonies, concerts, and college lectures are examples of _____.
        a.   conventional crowds
        b.   casual crowds
        c.   conventional aggregates
        d.   primary groups

16.   Worshipers at religious revival services; mourners lining the streets when a celebrity, public official, or religious leader has died; and revelers assembled at Mardi Gras are examples of _____.
        a.   acting crowds
        b.   conventional aggregates
        c.   primary groups
        d.   expressive crowds

17.   Lynchings, fire bombings, and effigy hangings are often carried out by _____.
        a.   casual crowds
        b.   expressive crowds
        c.   mobs
        d.   aggregates

18.   According to sociologist John Lofland, collective behavior may also be distinguished by the _____, which is the publicly expressed feeling perceived by participants and observers as the most prominent in an episode of collective behavior.
        a.   dominant emotion
        b.   dominant feeling
        c.   crowd personality type
        d.   mass personality type

19. According to John Lofland, fear, hostility and joy are three _____ that are often found in collective behavior.
    a. dominant emotions
    b. dominant feelings
    c. crowd personality types
    d. mass personality types

20. A(n) _____ is a collection of people who happen to be in the same place at the same time but who share little else in common.
    a. crowd
    b. mass
    c. institution
    d. aggregate

21. According to Herbert Blumer's typology, _____ are made up of people who come together for a scheduled event and thus share a common focus.
    a. casual crowds
    b. conventional crowds
    c. social institutions
    d. aggregates

22. According to Herbert Blumer's typology, _____ are relatively large gatherings of people who happen to be in the same place at the same time; if they interact at all, it is only briefly .
    a. casual crowds
    b. conventional crowds
    c. expressive crowds
    d. acting crowds

23. According to Herbert Blumer, _____ provide opportunities for the expression of some strong emotion such as joy, excitement, or grief.
    a. acting crowds
    b. expressive crowds
    c. conventional crowds
    d. casual crowds

24. _____ are collectivities so intensely focused on a specific purpose or object that they may erupt into violent or destructive behavior.
    a. Casual crowds
    b. Conventional crowds
    c. Expressive crowds
    d. Acting crowds

25. Mobs, riots, and panics are examples of _____.
    a. casual crowds
    b. conventional crowds
    c. expressive crowds
    d. acting crowds

26. A(n) _____ is a highly emotional crowd whose members engage in, or are ready to engage in, violence against a specific target--a person, a category of people, or physical property.
    a. riot
    b. panic
    c. mob
    d. aggregate

27. A(n) _____ is violent crowd behavior that is fueled by deep-seated emotions but not directed at one specific target.
    a. riot
    b. panic
    c. mob
    d. aggregate

28. Sit-ins, marches, boycotts, blockades, and strikes are examples of _____.
    a. casual crowds
    b. conventional crowds
    c. expressive crowds
    d. protest crowds

29. Panics are _____.
    a. extremely common
    b. fairly common
    c. relatively rare
    d. nonexistent

30. In the 1960s, African American students and sympathetic whites used sit-ins to call attention to racial injustice and demand social change. This is an example of a _____.
    a. protest crowd
    b. panic
    c. riot
    d. casual crowd

31. _____ is nonviolent action that seeks to change a policy or law by refusing to comply with it.
    a. Mob action
    b. Civil disobedience
    c. Urban terrorism
    d. A riot

32. _____ suggests that, because of its anonymity, the crowd transforms individuals from rational beings into a single organism with a collective mind. People do things as a collectivity that they would never do alone.
    a. Convergence theory
    b. Contagion theory
    c. Emergent Norm theory
    d. New Social Movement theory

33. _____ suggests that emotions such as fear and hate spread through a crowd because people experience a decline in personal responsibility.
    a. Convergence theory
    b. Contagion theory
    c. Emergent Norm theory
    d. New Social Movement theory

34. According to Robert Park (1921), social unrest is transmitted by a process of _____, which is the interactive communication between persons such that the discontent of one person is communicated to another, who, in turn, reflects the discontent back to the first person.
    a. societal reaction
    b. labeling
    c. circular reaction
    d. nonverbal communication

35. The _____ of crowd behavior suggests that people with similar attributes find a collectivity of like-minded persons with whom they can express their underlying personal tendencies.
    a. convergence theory
    b. contagion theory
    c. emergent norm theory
    d. new social movement theory

36. Hadley Cantril (1941) found that the participants in a lynching were poor and working-class whites who felt that their status was threatened by successful African Americans. Cantril's analysis is an example of _____.
    a. convergence theory
    b. contagion theory
    c. emergent norm theory
    d. new social movement theory

37. Sociologist Steven E. Clayman (1993) found that members of an audience listening to a speech applaud promptly and independently but wait to coordinate their booing with other people; they do not wish to "boo" alone. Clayman's research is most closely allied with which of the following theoretical approaches?
    a.   convergence theory
    b.   contagion theory
    c.   emergent norm theory
    d.   new social movement theory

38. According to _____, crowds develop their own definition of a situation and establish norms for behavior that fit the occasion.
    a.   convergence theory
    b.   contagion theory
    c.   emergent norm theory
    d.   new social movement theory

39. Rumors thrive when _____.
    a.   tensions are low
    b.   tensions are high
    c.   little authentic information is available
    d.   (b and c only)

40. Proponents of _____ suggest that crowds are not irrational. Rather, new norms are developed in a rational way to fit the situation.
    a.   convergence theory
    b.   contagion theory
    c.   emergent norm theory
    d.   new social movement theory

41. _____ is collective behavior that takes place when people (who often are geographically separated from one another) respond to the same event in much the same way.
    a.   Crowd behavior
    b.   Social unrest
    c.   Convergency
    d.   Mass behavior

42. Rumors, gossip, mass hysteria, public opinion, fashions, and fads are examples of _____.
    a.   crowd behavior
    b.   social unrest
    c.   convergency
    d.   mass behavior

43. _____ is/are unsubstantiated reports on an issue or subject.
   a. Fashions
   b. Fads
   c. Rumors
   d. Gossip

44. _____ refer(s) to rumors about the personal lives of indivuals.
   a. Fashions
   b. Fads
   c. Mass hysteria
   d. Gossip

45. _____ is a form of dispersed collective behavior that occurs when a large number of people react with strong emotions and self-destructive behavior to a real or perceived threat.
   a. Fashions
   b. Fads
   c. Mass hysteria (panic)
   d. Gossip

46. In 1938, a radio program was interrupted by news that Martians had landed in New Jersey and were in the process of conquering Earth. Thousands of listeners were reported to have barricaded themselves in their storm cellars or attempted to flee their homes. The listeners' reaction is an example of _____.
   a. fashions
   b. fads
   c. mass hysteria (panic)
   d. gossip

47. A _____ is a temporary but widely copied activity enthusiastically followed by large numbers of people.
   a. fashion
   b. fad
   c. riot
   d. rumor

48. "Streaking"--students taking off their clothes and running naked in public during the 1970s--is an example of a _____.
   a. fashion
   b. fad
   c. riot
   d. rumor

49.   A _____ is a currently valued style of behavior, thinking, or appearance.
       a.   fashion
       b.   fad
       c.   riot
       d.   rumor

50.   Sociologist Thorstein Veblen (1967/1899) argued that _____ serves mainly to
       institutionalize conspicuous consumption among the wealthy.
       a.   fashion
       b.   fad
       c.   riot
       d.   rumor

51.   _____ consist(s) of the attitudes and beliefs communicated by ordinary citizens to
       decision makers.
       a.   Propaganda
       b.   Culture
       c.   Public opinion
       d.   Election polls

52.   _____ is information provided by individuals or groups that have a vested interest
       in furthering their own cause or damaging an opposing one.
       a.   Propaganda
       b.   Culture
       c.   Public opinion
       d.   Election polls

53.   Initially, most grass-roots environmental activists attempt to influence _____ so
       that local decision makers will feel the necessity of correcting a specific problem through
       changes in public policy.
       a.   propaganda
       b.   culture
       c.   public opinion
       d.   political parties

54.   A(n) _____ is an organized group that acts consciously to promote or resist change
       through collective action.
       a.   social movement
       b.   collective movement
       c.   social structure
       d.   collective structure

55. The organized civil rights efforts by African Americans and others in the 1950s and 1960s is an example of a _____.
   a. social movement
   b. collective movement
   c. social structure
   d. collective structure

56. _____ movements seek to improve society by changing some specific aspect of the social structure.
   a. Resistance
   b. Revolutionary
   c. Alternative
   d. Reform

57. _____ movements seek limited change in some aspect of people's behavior. In the early twentieth century, for example, the Women's Christian Temperance Union attempted to get people to abstain from drinking alcoholic beverages.
   a. Resistance
   b. Revolutionary
   c. Alternative
   d. Reform

58. _____ movements (also referred to as *regressive movements*) seek to prevent change or to undo change that has already occurred. For example, Operation Rescue seeks to close abortion clinics.
   a. Resistance
   b. Revolutionary
   c. Alternative
   d. Reform

59. _____ seek to bring about a total change in society; they aim to remake the system by replacing existing institutions with new ones.
   a. Resistance
   b. Revolutionary
   c. Alternative
   d. Reform

60. _____ is the calculated unlawful use of physical force or threats of violence against persons or property in order to intimidate or coerce a government, organization, or individual for the purpose of gaining some political, religious, economic, or social objective.
   a. Resistance
   b. Civil disobedience
   c. Delinquency
   d. Terrorism

61. Hare Krishnas, the Unification Church, Scientology, and the Divine Light Mission all tend to appeal to the psychological and social needs of young people seeking meaning in life. They are examples of _____ movements.
    a. Religious
    b. Revolutionary
    c. Alternative
    d. Reform

62. In the _____ stage of development of social movements, an organizational structure develops, and a paid staff (rather than volunteers) begins to lead the group.
    a. preliminary (incipient)
    b. coalescence
    c. institutionalization (bureaucratization)
    d. (none of the above)

63. In the _____ stage of development of social movements, widespread unrest is present as people begin to become aware of a problem. Leaders emerge to agitate others into taking action.
    a. preliminary (incipient)
    b. coalescence
    c. institutionalization (bureaucratization)
    d. (none of the above)

64. According to _____, social movements arise because of people's perception that they have been deprived of their "fair share."
    a. value-added theory
    b. relative-deprivation theory
    c. resource mobilization theory
    d. new social movement theory

65. _____ refers to the discontent that people may feel when they compare their achievements with those of similarly situated persons and find that they have less than they think they deserve.
    a. Objective deprivation
    b. Poverty
    c. Relative deprivation
    d. Cultural capital

66. _____ assumes that widespread discontent alone cannot produce a social movement; adequate resources and motivated people are essential to any concerted social action.
    a. Value-added theory
    b. Relative-deprivation theory
    c. Resource mobilization theory
    d. New social movement theory

67. In Erving Goffman's book *Frame Analysis* (1974), he suggests that our interpretation of the particulars of events and activities is dependent on the framework from which we perceive them. Goffman's work is an example of _____.
   a.   Value-added theory
   b.   Relative-deprivation theory
   c.   Resource mobilization theory
   d.   Social constructionist theory

68. _____ is based on the assumption that a social movement is an interactive, symbolically defined, and negotiated process that involves participants, opponents and bystanders.
   a.   Value-added theory
   b.   Relative-deprivation theory
   c.   Resource mobilization theory
   d.   Social constructionist theory

69. The focus of _____ is on sources of social movements, including politics, ideology, and culture. Race, class, gender, sexuality, and other sources of identity are also factors in movements such as ecofeminism and environmental justice.
   a.   new social movement theory
   b.   relative-deprivation theory
   c.   resource mobilization theory
   d.   social constructionist theory

70. _____ is the belief that a disproportionate number of hazardous facilities (including industries such as waste disposal/treatment and chemical plants) are placed in low-income areas populated primarily by people of color.
   a.   Environmental redlining
   b.   Environmental inequality
   c.   Environmental racism
   d.   Environmental stratification

71. Which of the following is mentioned in your textbook as a factor that--in addition to collective behavior and social movements--contributes to social change?
   a.   the physical environment
   b.   population trends
   c.   technological development
   d.   (all of the above)

72. Which of the following is referred to in your textbook as a *natural disaster*?
   a.   hurricanes
   b.   tornados
   c.   floods
   d.   (all of the above)

73. It is estimated that about _____ of topsoil is lost annually due to soil erosion and other degradation of grazing land.
   a. 2.4 million tons
   b. 24 million tons
   c. 2.4 billion tons
   d. 24 billion tons

74. Which of the following has been a trend in the United States in recent years?
   a. a shift in population away from central cities
   b. a shrinking tax base in central cities
   c. an increase in the older population
   d. (all of the above)

75. Sociologist William Ogburn suggests that when a change in the material culture occurs in society, a period of _____ follows in which the nonmaterial (ideological) culture has not caught up with material development.
   a. developmental delay
   b. cultural lag
   c. cultural slowdown
   d. developmental disunity

True-False Questions

1. People's political and social behavior concerning environmental issues always conforms to their attitudes about these issues.

2. The presence of a relatively large number of people in the same location nearly always produces some form of collective behavior.

3. Mob violence tends to dissipate quickly once a target has been injured, killed, or destroyed.

4. Acts of civil disobedience may become violent; in this case, a protest crowd becomes an *acting crowd*.

5. Most social movements rely primarily on paid activists rather than volunteers to do the work that is required to advance the cause of the social movement.

6. Organized and large-scale efforts to change public policy regarding abortion, womens' rights, gun control, and environmental justice may be classified as *social movements*.

7. The 1995 bombing of the Federal Building in Oklahoma City is an example of *domestic terrorism*.

When a social movement reaches the *institutionalization* or *bureaucratization* stage, there is a danger of its members losing their initial zeal and idealism as administrators take over management of the organization.

9. According to Neil Smelser's *value-added theory*, if there is a high level of social control on the part of law enforcement officials, political leaders, and others, it becomes much easier to develop a social movement.

10. One of the major problems in the world today is ensuring an adequate supply of potable water.

11. In many high-income nations of the world, medical advances have increased the human lifespan.

12. One of the major changes that took place in the U.S. during the twentieth century was a dramatic rise in the number of two-parent families.

13. The United States was one of the last nations in the world to provide universal education of young people, regardless of their ability to pay.

14. *Riparian rights* refers to the rights of a person or group to use the land (but not the water) on the shore of a body of water.

15. An *acquifer* is an underground water supply.

Chapter 16: Answers to Practice Test Questions

(question-answer-page)

Multiple Choice Questions

1. d 463
2. c 463
3. c 464
4. d 464
5. d 464
6. d 464
7. d 464
8. b 465
9. a 465
10. a 465
11. b 465
12. d 466
13. a 466
14. b 467
15. a 467
16. d 467
17. c 467
18. a 467
19. a 467
20. d 467
21. b 467
22. a 467
23. b 467
24. d 467
25. d 467
26. c 467
27. a 468
28. d 468
29. c 468
30. a 469
31. b 469
32. b 469
33. b 469
34. c 469
35. a 469
36. a 469
37. c 470
38. c 470
39. d 471
40. c 471
41. d 471
42. d 471
43. c 471
44. d 471
45. c 472
46. c 472
47. b 472
48. b 472
49. a 473
50. a 473
51. c 473
52. a 473
53. c 474
54. a 474
55. a 475
56. d 475
57. c 476
58. a 477
59. b 476
60. d 476
61. a 476
62. c 477
63. a 477
64. b 478
65. c 478
66. c 480
67. d 480
68. d 480
69. a 483
70. c 482
71. d 482
72. d 482
73. d 483
74. d 485
75. b 485

True-False Questions

1. F 465
2. F 467
3. T 468
4. T 469
5. F 474
6. T 475
7. T 476
8. T 478
9. F 479
10. T 483
11. T 485
12. F 485
13. F 485
14. F 487
15. T 487